Common-Sense
Classroom Management

CORWIN PRESS

The Corwin Press logo—a raven striding across an open book—represents the happy union of courage and learning. We are a professional-level publisher of books and journals for K-12 educators, and we are committed to creating and providing resources that embody these qualities. Corwin's motto is "Success for All Learners."

Common-Sense
Classroom Management

**Surviving September and Beyond
in the Elementary Classroom**

Jill A. Lindberg • April M. Swick

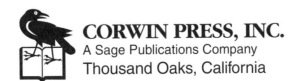

CORWIN PRESS, INC.
A Sage Publications Company
Thousand Oaks, California

For information:

Corwin Press, Inc.
A Sage Publications Company
2455 Teller Road
Thousand Oaks, California 91320
E-mail: order@corwinpress.com

Sage Publications Ltd.
6 Bonhill Street
London EC2A 4PU
United Kingdom

Sage Publications India Pvt. Ltd.
M-32 Market
Greater Kailash I
New Delhi 110 048 India

Printed in the United States of America

Library of Congress Cataloging-in-Publication Data

Lindberg, Jill.
    Common-sense classroom management: Surviving September and beyond
in the elementary classroom / by Jill A. Lindberg and April M. Swick.
        p. cm.
    Includes bibliographical references and index.
        ISBN 0-7619-7885-2 (c: acid-free paper) — ISBN 0-7619-7886-0 (p: acid-free paper)
        1. Classroom management—United States. 2. Elementary school
teaching—United States.   I. Swick, April M. II. Title.
    LB3013 .L55 2002
    372.1102'4—dc21

                          2001002908

01   02   03   04   05   06   07   7   6   5   4   3   2   1

Acquiring Editor: Faye Zucker
Corwin Editorial Assistant: Julia Parnell
Production Editor: Olivia Weber
Editorial Assistant: Kathryn Journey
Typesetter/Designer: Larry K. Bramble
Cover Designer: Michael Dubowe
Indexer: Molly Hall

■ Contents

■ Foreword

When considering practices that foster effective classroom management, several thoughts come to mind. Some familiar mantras heard lately include: effective management is proactive; effective management uses an instructional approach; effective classroom management always respects the dignity of the individual. While few would choose to counter such notions, the single most important element that leads to sound classroom management can be summarized in two words: *common sense*.

What constitutes common sense, however, is not always that obvious. And finding those subtle means to put common-sense strategies into practice can be an elusive goal, even for the most experienced of teachers. Consider the following examples. Most would recognize the use of proximity control as a useful way to discourage a chatty student. But creating physical pathways to facilitate this strategy is perhaps less apparent. Most teachers know that they should post rules and refer to them as needed. But they might not realize how eye contact, body language, and facial expressions can avert a rule violation without a word being uttered.

Common-Sense Classroom Management: Surviving September and Beyond in the Elementary Classroom by Jill Lindberg and April Swick addresses these types of behavioral nuances with concrete, concise, and practical tips for educators. It provides a fresh perspective and keen insight into dealing with the increased rates of attention and behavioral deficits that characterize modern society. It provides constructive and beneficial advice for teachers willing to go that extra mile to implement sound practice, while recognizing the fact that they have precious little time to steep themselves in the theoretical arena.

Means-tested by the authors during a lifetime of urban teaching, this volume brings a new dimension and a deeper perspective to the term *common sense* as it relates to classroom management. And in doing so, it brings to educators an indispensable tool to identify and put into practice those subtle changes that collectively make a difference in the atmosphere of a classroom.

Anthony Pedriana
Principal, Twenty-First Street Elementary School
Milwaukee, Wisconsin

■ Preface

Dear Teacher,

This book—really a manual of sorts—is a proactive, common-sense approach to help you create a successful classroom learning environment. The strategies you find here can be implemented without extensive interpretation or planning, creation of materials, or permission from your administrator. They cover all aspects of a typical school day, providing specific and very practical ideas to assist in solving your classroom management problems.

We realize, of course, that schools vary from city to city and system to system. We know, however, that many needs and concerns are common to all teachers no matter where they are. We think you will recognize some of your own needs and concerns in this book.

We have taken care to make this book very user-friendly. Each strategy is limited to five points or fewer, and April Swick's drawings illustrate some of the ideas. A *light bulb icon* appears wherever the strategy has been adapted for younger students. An *IDEA icon* indicates a strategy that can be adapted for use with special education students; IDEA is an acronym for the Individuals with Disabilities Education Act of 1997 (P. L. No. 105-17; 20 U.S.C. § 1401).

Keep in mind that these ideas can and should be changed or modified to fit your particular classroom situation. They are not written in stone and should be seen only as a means to an end in assisting you to develop the classroom management system that will serve you and your students best.

This book is a great resource—whether you're a new elementary school teacher, a new teacher trainer, or a mentor teacher. These clear, easy-to-implement strategies will help you or a colleague plan an effective management program that will help ensure ongoing success in your classroom.

Have a great school year!

Sincerely,

Jill A. Lindberg
April M. Swick

■ Acknowledgments

We thank our friend and colleague, Mrs. Georgia Janza, master teacher now retired, for her significant contribution to this book. Without her invaluable input, we would not have been able to apply our management strategies to kindergarten and first-grade classrooms.

The contributions of the following reviewers are also gratefully acknowledged:

Anita Perry
First-Grade Teacher, St. Bernadette's Catholic School
Northboro, MA

Betsy McTear
Educational Consultant, Adjunct Faculty, Sussex County Community College
Newton, NJ

Michelle Kocar
Sixth-Grade Science and Math Teacher, Parkside Intermediate School
Westlake, OH

Mildred Murray-Ward
Professor of Education, California Lutheran University
Thousand Oaks, CA

■ About the Authors

Jill A. Lindberg has a BS in Exceptional Education from the University of Wisconsin–Milwaukee. She is currently a special education mentor teacher working with first-year special education teachers affiliated with the University of Wisconsin–Milwaukee/Milwaukee Public Schools Special Education Internship Program. She has also been a mentor with the Milwaukee Teachers' Education Association/Milwaukee Public Schools Mentor Teacher Program and has worked with both special education and regular education teachers. Other experience includes 3 years working with learning disabled students in a full-inclusion setting as well as 5 years as a teacher of emotionally, behaviorally disordered students in Milwaukee public schools. In addition, she spent 4 years in the Madison, Wisconsin, public school system teaching hearing impaired children.

Although special education is her first love, her experience as a mentor has encouraged an interest in working with adult learners. Assisting first-year educators as they develop their skills has given her surprising insight into the need for basic classroom management strategies such as the ones in this book.

April M. Swick was assigned to Clement Avenue Elementary School, Milwaukee, Wisconsin, in August 1990 and began with a class of combined fourth and fifth graders. She was a highly involved staff member, concerned not only with the success of the children in her classroom but also with the betterment of the entire school population. She belonged to a wide variety of committees and worked to ensure schoolwide discipline, a positive climate, and school spirit. After teaching for several more years, she and her current coauthor and friend, Jill Lindberg, became the first full-inclusion teaching team in the school.

In the fall of 2001, she was appointed assistant principal of Clement Avenue School. She has earned a master's degree plus 32 additional credits from the University of Wisconsin–Milwaukee, and she intends to pursue a doctorate in education. She would love to write and illustrate children's books. Sharing her good ideas with young teachers and a principalship are also future goals.

This book is dedicated to my mother,
who has been a guide and support for me always.

Jill Lindberg

I would like to dedicate this book to all my family,
friends, and colleagues whose constant support,
encouragement, and love made this book possible.

April Swick

Taking Care of Teacher Business

Taking care of yourself as a teacher within your classroom is of utmost importance. Don't minimize the value of feeling organized and in control of your school day. Think of yourself as the lead actor on your classroom stage—you are the one who keeps the unfolding drama on track. If you haven't rehearsed your lines well and made sure all your props are in place, your little way-off-Broadway production will be a flop.

Chapter Outline

- Room Organization
- Teacher Desk Organization
- Planning
- Independent Activities While Teacher Works With Small Groups
- Reviewing Expectations
- Field Trips
- Making the Most of Your Paraprofessional Assistant

Room Organization

Stumped as to why *Sesame Street* turns into *Jerry Springer*? Frustrated when free time becomes a free-for-all? Perhaps it's time to change the channel—and the room arrangement—to encourage academic progress and squelch sassy behavior before it starts.

▶ 1. Your first task is to find a success-oriented seating arrangement for your students (see Chapter 2 under the heading Classroom Seating on page 11). Once you have decided on this, it's important to realize that the arrangement of the remainder of the furniture is also key to classroom harmony. No matter how you choose to group desks, computers, reading materials, or activity centers, provide a clear travel path for you and your students to reach all work areas in the room.

▶ 2. Be sure you have a clear view of the entire classroom from anywhere you may be working. Avoid the possibility of misadventure by keeping everyone in your line of sight.

▶ 3. Conversely, be sure the entire class has an unobstructed view of you as well as the chalkboard, overhead projections, or any other visuals you may be using to teach a lesson. Students who cannot see what is happening quickly find other things to absorb their attention. Also note that when deciding on your seating plan, you should consider children who may have hearing or sight problems or other difficulties that might affect their ability to concentrate. Monitor this all during the school year, because changes often accompany physical growth in children.

▶ 4. Remember that a neat, orderly room sets a good example for your students regarding their own desks and schoolwork. Resist the temptation to fill every open space with clutter. Clean up after activities that produce disarray—or better yet, give students the responsibility. (See Chapter 2 under the heading Classroom Monitors and Jobs on page 16.) Make it a point to leave your room neat and clean at day's end. It helps to set a positive tone for both you and your students the next morning.

▶ 5. As soon as you detect a problem regarding room arrangement, fix it. Sometimes, just a few minutes spent to adjust a screen, move a desk or table, or reorganize an activity center can eliminate potential classroom difficulties.

Teacher Desk Organization

If you admit—only to yourself, of course—that you have never seen the top of your desk, that you are sure the mound you face daily must be reproducing itself, then you need to get organized quickly. If you haven't a clue as to how you can do so, read on.

▶ 1. Think about the items you find on your desk and put them into categories. For example: communications from the office, notes from parents, homework, notes to yourself, and so forth—you might choose different ones. Then decide how you will file these things in a way that makes sense. You may use wire baskets, file folders, colored pocket folders, or another method—whatever works for you. Label them so you will be sure to put your papers in the appropriate place.

▶ 2. Most desks have at least one file drawer. Use such a drawer to file little-needed items such as school catalogues or other things you may want to keep but don't use often. Use another drawer as a catchall—a place to hold any items that don't fit neatly into your desk organization plan. But remember to inventory this drawer frequently to discard things or find a permanent home for them.

▶ 3. See what's left on your desk. Do you find paperclips, pencils, rubber bands, non-school-related items taken from students? You need to find a home in your desk drawer for these things. Take a look in there—did you recoil in horror? If so, get organized. You can buy inexpensive plastic containers of various shapes to hold all the miscellaneous desk supplies now cluttering the top of your desk; or use small cardboard boxes. If you want some items, such as pencils, pens, and paperclips on your desk, then get a cup for writing tools, a holder for your paperclips, and so forth.

▶ 4. Now that you are organized, the most important thing to remember is to make it a practice to use your new system regularly until it becomes a habit. Your plan is only as good as your ability to implement it. If you find you have little time during the day to put things in their appropriate places, take 5 minutes during lunch and then another 5 minutes at the end of the day to regroup.

▶ 5. Try not to leave school without cleaning up your desk and placing things you'll need for tomorrow front and center. You'll be amazed at how good it feels to come in the next day to a neat desk with the day's agenda ready to tackle.

Planning

Do you white-knuckle your way through the school day as you and your students ride the daily schedule roller coaster? Do unplanned twists and turns churn your stomach into knots? Calm down—here's a soothing remedy for that queasy feeling.

▶ 1. *Don't underestimate the importance of written lesson plans.* Experienced as well as new teachers need them to provide a sense of direction and speed for the week. Also, someday soon your principal will come looking for them—guaranteed. Equally important is the day you wake up unexpectedly with the flu. Knowing your completed lesson plans are on your desk for your substitute will calm both you and your administrator. Be aware also that it's a dangerous idea to wait too long to prepare your complete substitute teacher folder—absences can be very unexpected.

▶ 2. Most teachers—new and veteran—experience frustration with the ever-changing, all-school schedule, special classes, and other interrupters to their day. The first thing to remember is this: The only thing certain in your day is that nothing is certain. Once you can accept that fact, you can begin to bring some order to your schedule.

▶ 3. One helpful way to begin to organize is to open your weekly lesson plan book and enter everything that you know is already scheduled for the week in question. Put in recess, music, art, gym, any programs or other all-school activities, and so forth. If your school has set blocks of time for certain academic areas such as reading and math, include them. Then note the times that specific students are gone from your classroom for whatever reason. You may even want to enter these things with a colored pen or pencil so they are quickly visible to you.

▶ 4. Once you've done this, you can clearly identify the times remaining to be used for academic lessons, and you can add them to your plans. There will be weeks, during holiday periods or other special events, when teaching time will be at a premium. Laying out your schedule in this way allows you to maximize available teaching time for the benefit of your students.

▶ 5. Until you get a sense for what your class can accomplish in a given amount of time, *overplan*. Completing a lesson the next day is much preferred to finding yourself stuck with dead air to fill. If this does happen, you will want to have a contingency plan (see Chapter 4 under the heading If a Lesson Really Isn't Working on page 35). Also be sure to include ideas for quiet, orderly transition times (see Chapter 5, Transitioning). Often the success of your plan rises or falls on how well your group can transition from one activity to the next.

Independent Activities While Teacher Works With Small Groups

Does the phrase *ringmaster in a three-ring circus* come to mind as you juggle small groups, students at their desks, and the various comings and goings in your classroom? If you think a whip and a chair are the only things to bring order to this chaos, give these suggestions a try.

▶ 1. Begin by thinking about your particular classroom situation. Are you teaching second grade or fifth grade? Are you alone all day or do you have an aide some of the time? Do you have access to any adult volunteer assistance? What are the dynamics of your classroom? Do you have several behaviorally or academically challenging students? All of these variables are factors in deciding how you will plan your large and small group work.

▶ 2. One of the most challenging scenarios involves a younger group of children and no assistant in your classroom. You need to plan independent work for the large group while you teach a small group. Seatwork packets can be very useful if they are well thought out. These consist of three or four stapled pages of a variety of tasks that your students can complete with initial directions but little or no follow-up assistance from you. You can find many good workbooks in teacher supply stores addressing myriad academic skills, which can be resources for your work packets.

▶ 3. These packets can address such areas as math, language arts, writing, spelling, critical thinking, or anything else you feel is valuable. Some teachers include board work with the packet or add it for students who work faster. A key element is that the work must be within the capability of students to do on their own. Another important factor is to keep the work similar from day to day so that your directions are familiar. Vastly different work each day can cost you precious time giving and reiterating directions and can produce confusion and repeated questions from your students. Remember to have quiet work choices for students who finish early, such as reading, journaling, completing unfinished assignments, and so forth.

▶ 4. Seatwork of this type can be a valuable instructional tool—do not view it as busywork. It teaches individual responsibility, good listening, careful following of directions, and ability to work independently. It can also provide a good academic review of skills you are teaching. Of course, all of this depends on your class being held responsible for the work. If students are not held accountable, the assignments will be meaningless. Be sure to take time to grade the work, and discuss it at least several times a week with your class.

▶ 5. You can use this same concept with older students, with some variations. Often, upper-grade students have unfinished classroom or homework assignments to complete, which occupy their time while you work with a small group. Work packets can be used as extra credit. A larger number of more challenging work pages can be included. Students can be given an entire week to complete these at their own pace to earn extra points. Older students often enjoy the challenge of managing and completing work they choose to do.

For special education students, consult with the special education teacher about what you plan to assign for independent work. The special education teacher may need to work with you to modify the activities so they are appropriate for the skill level of these students. Also, depending on the form of service delivery your school uses for special education students, the special education teacher may be in your classroom and use independent work time either to assist students with the work or to make sure they are up-to-date with other assignments.

Reviewing Expectations

Do you wish you had a tape recorder as you verbally replay your directions and classroom expectations? Remember: Persistence pays off—even if it means hitting the rewind button again and again. These useful suggestions will reap long-term benefits.

▶ 1. Clearly post your classroom rules. (See Chapter 6 under the heading Classroom Rules on page 59.) Make them a living document by quoting them frequently to your students. Remember to state them in a positive manner, such as, "I am pleased to see Jerrell is keeping his hands and feet to himself." By doing so, you send two messages: Your classroom rules matter, and you notice when your students are complying with them. The more often you do this, the more significant your rules will become.

▶ 2. Avoid forcing students to write rules as punishment. They become meaningless if used in this manner. In addition, writing should be viewed as a positive pursuit rather than a negative chore. Instead, ask the student to read the ignored rule and to remind the class why this rule was agreed on. Then continue with your teaching—don't belabor the issue. Also be sensitive to occasional slips by otherwise well-behaved students.

▶ 3. If a child repeatedly has difficulty with a particular expectation, meet with the child to discuss possible solutions. Be sure to give the student ownership of the answer by expecting participation in deciding what will be done. In turn, when you observe this student following the rule—or any of the classroom rules—be quick to offer a compliment.

▶ 4. Remind your class that behavior expectations follow them out of your classroom to wherever they may go within the building, on the playground, on the bus, or in the community. Reviewing your rules should be an important part of preparing your class to venture outside their classroom door, especially during the first several months of a new school year. Random praise and rewards for exemplary individual—as well as whole-class—behavior encourages students to make positive choices.

► 5. Expectations for classroom work go hand in hand with behavior expectations and are equally important. Provide samples of work that exemplify your highest standards. Post examples of how you expect papers to be headed. Compliment a job well done. Discuss poor quality work with the whole class if many are guilty; otherwise, speak individually to the offending students. Monitor your class as they work, by walking from desk to desk and commenting on work caliber. Be aware that quality of work may slip as the year progresses, and you may need to review expectations several times. Set standards for long-term projects; be sure your class understands them. Review them throughout the project. Remember—all of these suggestions will work *only* if you make your students accountable for them.

Field Trips

Would you rather stick pins under your fingernails than take your class on a field trip? If the mere thought of organizing one of these adventures and then actually carrying through gives you nightmares, take heart. It can be done with some simple but thorough preplanning.

► 1. Get a jump on your field trip schedule by gathering information on potential outings as soon as possible—even as early as late spring for the following year if you know about your future class. Begin to compile a field trip folder, and keep any information you gather for future reference, including your own comments regarding successes, failures, and changes to be made.

► 2. Create a blanket field trip permission slip that can be used for any outing. Then all you need to do is fill in the blanks with current information. Make ample extra copies because some students will misplace theirs—perhaps more than once. Be sure to send the slips home with students well in advance, and provide daily reminders to return them. If money is involved, be sure you know your school's policy regarding students who, for whatever reason, do not pay. If a child has forgotten the permission slip on the day of the trip, confer with your school administration as to whether a call to the parent for permission will suffice. Do not make this decision yourself.

► 3. Discuss particulars of the trip thoroughly, several times, with your class. Cover provisions for lunch—will the school provide it, or will students need to bring their own? If the trip is outdoors or requires special clothing, be sure to address this. Don't assume children will know how to dress appropriately either for the weather or for the type of trip. Be sure your students are very clear about your rules during the trip. Discuss bus behavior and potentially inappropriate actions during the trip. You may even need to designate an adult helper to be available to sit with any disruptive students. Discuss your safety concerns—students should always be where they can see their chaperone and where their chaperone can see them.

▶ 4. Do not underestimate your need for enough adult supervision. Doing so could compromise safety as well as enjoyment of the trip. You should plan one adult to no more than four children for younger-age groups and a ratio of one to five or six with older students. This, of course, also depends on student behavior and maturity level. You may also want to consider using nametags, which include the school name and phone number, for younger children.

▶ 5. Here are a few final but crucial reminders. Be sure all arrangements for payment for bus, admission, and any other expenses have been completed before the trip. Complications here could spoil the excursion for everyone. If your outing is dependent on good weather, have an alternate in-school plan in case inclement weather forces you to cancel the trip. Be sure you know the exact number of students you have taken, and *count* them before you get on the bus to return to school. Children have been known to be left behind.

Making the Most of Your Paraprofessional Assistant

Are you one of the lucky ones who has a paraprofessional or an educational assistant just begging for your direction and guidance? Not sure, though, where or how to direct someone over three feet tall? Once again, thoughtful preparation is the key.

▶ 1. Never assume your paraprofessional or assistant has had formal training or practical experience directing or controlling children. Remember that this person is a helper to you and your class. Plan the aide's time so that he or she works under your guidance, especially at first. This will allow you to observe how the aide takes direction and carries it out as well as how the aide relates to your students. Be aware that your aide is not a surrogate teacher. Having one in your classroom is not meant to free you to sit at your desk or to go to the teachers' lounge.

▶ 2. If you feel uncomfortable giving directions and orchestrating your helper's every move, prepare a schedule. If possible, do this together to foster a sense of partnership. Your assistant may provide some valuable insight as to how best to support you. Be sure you have the supplies and materials ready for your helper's assigned task. If your assistant is working separately from you, always have one eye and one ear open in that direction so that if problems arise, you can step in quickly.

▶ 3. If you feel tension building between you and your assistant, for whatever reason, address the problem as soon as possible. Waiting too long can only make it worse and lessen the chance of getting your professional relationship back on track. If your helper is unresponsive to your fence-mending efforts, you may need to seek the advice of a school administrator. But choose this route only if your personal efforts have failed. Also remember that praise and thanks are very inexpensive ways to maintain cordial relations. Try not to let a day go by without offering a word of appreciation for a job well done.

▶ 4. Maintaining a united front with your assistant as you work with your class during the school day is extremely important. Disagreeing in front of your students is unprofessional. Your helper should be clear about your classroom expectations and should abide by your decisions. If your assistant deviates, don't use time in front of your class to debate the issue. Discuss it privately—and remember to listen to the assistant's side. Your helper may have some valuable insight into the situation.

▶ 5. Your school may also have general aides to do clerical tasks, including copying materials for teachers. In addition to your school secretary and the engineer, you will want to be good friends with this person. One way you can do this is by following your school's guidelines for submitting materials to be copied. These will probably include providing clear directions as to how you want your materials completed and submitting them well in advance of your need for them. Remember that you are not the only one in your school using the services of this person. Your understanding when problems occur, and your willingness to show appreciation for good service, can help put you on this aide's favorite-teacher list.

Creating a Positive Classroom Atmosphere

Every teacher understands the importance of promoting and maintaining a positive classroom atmosphere. Each school is a microcosm of our society, with its positives and negatives, and the importance of creating cohesiveness through respect, honesty, kindness, and courtesy among our students can't be minimized. The strategies included in this chapter offer some ways to begin to do this within your own classroom. Combine these ideas with some of those appearing in the chapters on rewards and negative consequences to help your family of students live and learn together successfully all year long.

Chapter Outline

- Classroom Seating
- Decorating With Themes
- Connecting With Parents—Classroom Newsletters
- Classroom Monitors and Jobs
- Respect in Your Classroom
- Super Student of the Week
- Classroom Meetings
- Compliment Book
- Wall of Fame
- Tattling

Classroom Seating

Too close for comfort—does this phrase ring a bell when you think of the seating arrangements for some students in your class? Here's a painless way to relieve those seating-chart blues.

▶ 1. During the first few days of school, most teachers allow students to sit at whatever desk they like. This provides a good opportunity to see how students influence one another and to plan a more scientific seating arrangement.

▶ 2. Over the first few days, observe student interactions. For example:

    a. Look for students who seem to be doing too much talking.

    b. Look for students who seem to be annoying, provoking, or tattling on each other.

    c. Look for students who are quiet, cooperative, and mind their own business.

    d. Look for students who seem helpful to others.

▶ 3. You may want to jot some brief comments on your class list to remind yourself of the qualities that certain students possess. Then draw a seating chart based on your classroom arrangement—whether it's single desks, groups of desks, single tables, or tables moved together. Look at the personality make-up of your class, and seat students so that talkers sit close to those who are quiet and focused, students who annoy or provoke are near those who can ignore and be quiet, and students who can never find the right page are paired with a Mr. or Ms. Helpful.

▶ 4. Remind those students who moan and complain about the changes you make that future seating will depend on good behavior, and those who can show maturity may be able to have some input as to where they will sit.

▶ 5. Be aware that you may need to change the seating arrangement in your classroom several times during the year. Even the best combinations can become weary of one another if they are together too long. You may also want to change the configuration of the desks or tables in your room a few times during the year. These changes can breathe new life into classroom combinations that have become tiresome and problematic.

In kindergarten or early primary classes, some teachers do assign permanent spots at tables. Many teachers at this level, however, choose to give the children the freedom to decide where they will work, because socialization and decision-making skills are important goals.

If you have special education students in you classroom, you may want to consider strategic seating for them. Depending on their needs, you may want them seated near you, or you may want them next to a student who could help them with academic work when possible. If they have challenging behavior, you may want to seat them next to a student who can be a role model of appropriate behavior.

Decorating With Themes

Worried you'll have to hire an interior decorator to make a good first impression on all those shiny little faces crowding into your classroom on the first day? Never fear—there's an easier way.

▶ 1. Choose a theme for the year: heroes, environment, space, dinosaurs, Disney movies, popular cartoons—the possibilities are infinite. Then decide what you want to portray and how it can fit into your classroom decorating areas. Remember to leave adequate bulletin board space to display your students' good work also.

▶ 2. Not an artist? That problem can be solved in several ways. Teaching supply stores have an ever-increasing collection of thematic materials. Decide on a theme in advance, and buy a little at a time to avoid a big strain on your pocketbook. Some schools may have monies available for you to use for classroom purchases. Thinking ahead can also involve creating your theme materials by enlarging and tracing them on your overhead—do it now for next year. Your students can even be involved. Buy simple coloring books for patterns; then paint and color them, cut them out, and finally, laminate them for posterity.

▶ 3. Whatever theme you choose, be sure it has high student interest and can be tied to positive classroom behavior. You may want to include some dialogue for the characters, or other messages to help promote good behavior, family atmosphere, respect, tolerance, hard work, academic excellence, and other good qualities. Remember, the theme should create enthusiasm and motivate students.

▶ 4. Be sure to save your themes from year to year by storing them in large, labeled folders for use with other classes. After a few years, you can recycle them, and they will be fresh and new to future students. In this way, you can develop new classroom theme ideas at your leisure while still making use of some of your original creations.

In kindergarten and early primary classes, it is important to have the room reflect the students who own the room and live there. One way to do this is to define your bulletin boards with boarders that reflect seasonal, academic, or holiday themes. Fill one with each cihild's self-portrait drawn on the first day to help show visitors who lives in your room. (Draw a picture of yourself to display also.) Me Mobiles made by the children, which include each child's face and name as well as favorite colors, interests, and so forth can decorate the room as well as build self-esteem. Be sure to include a birthday board to help celebrate each child's special day.

Arranging your room into activity centers for such subjects as math, writing, art, science, puzzles, and library can also be a way to make your room both utilitarian and attractive. Make or purchase large, attractive signs to help your students identify each activity center and to draw them to it. Be sure these are in place the first day so your children can identify and use your activity centers right away.

Connecting With Parents—Classroom Newsletters

When conference time rolls around, do parents you meet ask what's been going on in your classroom? According to their child, nothing is. A little time spent on a weekly family newsletter can be a painless and helpful solution.

▶ 1. A one-page, weekly, family newsletter can be an excellent communication vehicle. Some computer knowledge—possessed by most teachers—will suffice to create something useful and informative. You might want to have a classroom contest to name your paper. You could include a small student section offering those interested an opportunity to write about a topic of choice.

▶ 2. Configure your newsletter on a school or home computer. A two-column newspaper format works well. Save the skeleton format so you can simply add or delete student names, change the date, and update news and reminders.

▶ 3. Below are some suggestions for things to include in your weekly communiqué:

   a. A list of your Wall of Fame students for the week—kids love to see their name in print.

   b. Information on any upcoming field trips (especially any cost and due date for the money) or special classroom or schoolwide events—students may provide vague information on these things, but families want to know the details.

   c. Lists of needs for your classroom, whether for art projects, special studies, or even adults willing to share special skills, hobbies, or talents that fit with an area of study—you may be surprised how many families will respond to your requests.

   d. Include a few sentences each on what you're doing in math, reading, science, social studies, and other subjects—families feel good about teachers who keep them informed on an ongoing basis about academics.

▶ 4. Always distribute your newsletter on the same day each week. Doing this helps families know when to expect it—Fridays work out well. Your classroom meeting would be a great time to read it with your students so you can emphasize especially important items. Be sure it goes directly into each student's book bag to ensure a safe arrival home.

► 5. Keep a file of all of your newsletters. It can serve many useful purposes. Here are two ideas for next year: Compile a reference for any awards you may give at semester- or year-end to your Wall of Famers; keep a record of information sent home to parents—just in case someone says, "I was never informed about that." (This is a great method to let your principal know about another way you are reaching families; you might consider slipping a copy in the principal's mailbox each week.)

A newsletter for kindergarten and early primary children should encourage parents to have their children tell them about things they are learning—such as colors, numbers, poems, and favorite songs. This promotes language development and can also alert parents to learning problems if their children are consistently unable to verbalize what they have learned.

There are also a number of ways you can connect with the parents of the children in your class in addition to a newsletter. Plan some weekly independent work that has a child's creative input as well as curriculum or reading vocabulary so that the children are eager to share their work with parents—to reread it so that the facts or words are reinforced because of the children's pride in their product. Encourage parents to provide a space or box to save this work so that it can be read again and again.

Make your classroom a welcome place for family visitors or volunteers. You can familiarize them with your program, help them understand what goes on during their child's school day, and model some techniques for working with their child at home. They can also listen to children read, work on some individual math, or prepare materials for future projects.

Select some core items that can be copied for each child to take home on weekends or to keep at home during the length of time the class is working on a particular curriculum project. Secure them in book form or in a box to ensure they will not be lost or destroyed. Parents can see for themselves how their child is doing and can always have a way of helping their child at home.

Make projects and directions clear and simple. For example, create an alphabet book that includes the following: a place for the child to write the letter from a model, a poem containing words beginning with the target letter, and a place where the child can draw a picture of something beginning with the letter. These activities will address academic skills such as phonics, letter recognition, poetry memorizing, and language development.

wsy Notes

November 12, 2001

Wall of Fame

Congratulations to this week's
Wall of Famers!! You completed all your
homework, and were in school every day
last week. We are proud of you!! Keep up
the SUPER work!!

Sam Harmon

Jenny Smith

Maxwell Rios

Violet Marcks

Anthony Lesher

Rachel Evans

Harry Swick

Haley Sporek

Jack Olstinski

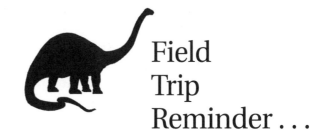

Field Trip Reminder . . .

Don't forget to turn in your
permission slips and $3.00 for our
upcoming field trip to the dinosaur
museum. We still have plenty of
room for chaperones, so be sure
to ask your parents if they will
be able to attend!

Book Order

The monthly book order is due
next Friday. Fill out your
order forms completely
and turn them in as
soon as possible.

Book Report Projects

All book report projects are due
on the last day of the month. I am
eager for each of you to share the
beautiful work you have done!

Classroom Monitors and Jobs

How do you keep organized without a secretary to help with all the paper and grunt work? Hire a responsible student or two to lighten your daily classroom load.

▶ 1. Once you've gotten your bearings and have established a daily routine, you may feel comfortable enough to enlist the help of your students with the myriad jobs and housekeeping chores that need to be done within your classroom.

▶ 2. Decide what jobs you must have done daily, and think about when and how you expect them to be completed. The following are examples of those that can be handled by students in the second grade and beyond: cleaning erasers, bringing out or in the playground equipment, washing boards and overheads, leading the line, changing the calendar, managing windows and shades, taking lunch count and attendance, handling supply orders, number-ordering homework, and helping with the classroom library or computers. Kindergarten students can assist in clean-up time throughout the room as well as help with lunch count and even attendance.

▶ 3. Spend time discussing and modeling your expectations for each classroom chore. Let your class know that students who are not responsible risk losing their positions. Devise a job application (Figure 2.2) and interview applicants for the various tasks. During the interview, elicit such information as past work experience (home chores), the reason they are applying for the position, and the reason they feel you should hire them.

▶ 4. Be sure to take the time to train new employees. You may want to devise very brief job descriptions. Have them sign a copy for you and one for them to keep. Be clear and specific about how you expect tasks to be completed. After a month or so, ask for new applicants, and hire a new set of employees. Limit each student to one classroom job so everyone has an opportunity to help.

▶ 5. Post job titles and employees in a highly visible spot that can be quickly referenced. If a student is chronically late, absent, or forgetful about a chore, reassign as necessary.

Respect in Your Classroom

Do things get stormy in your classroom too often? Harsh words exchanged between students or even (dare we say?) between students and teachers do little to foster a positive climate. Here are some ideas to calm those troubled waters.

▶ 1. It is *imperative* for you to *listen* when students talk to you. Students won't give you the respect you need to be effective in the classroom unless they feel you sincerely listen to and care about them. Impossible, you say? You'd be surprised at how much you can learn and how much trust you can gain by giving students just a few minutes of your undivided

Figure 2.2 Job Application for Students Who Want to Help in the Classroom

JOB APPLICATION

STUDENT NAME: _____

ROOM #: _____   GRADE: _____

DATE: _____

CIRCLE THE JOB THAT YOU ARE APPLYING FOR:

LIBRARIAN   SUPPLY ORDER   LUNCH COUNT
        BOARDS   WINDOWS   CADET   EQUIPMENT

ARE YOU A RESPONSIBLE PERSON WHO CAN GET TO SCHOOL ON TIME EVERY DAY AND WHO TRIES TO HAVE GOOD ATTENDANCE?
YES _____   NO _____

ABOUT HOW MANY DAYS HAVE YOU BEEN ABSENT? _____

DO YOU WANT TO HELP OTHERS?
YES _____   NO _____

HAVE YOU EVER BEEN SENT TO THE OFFICE FOR BREAKING ANY SCHOOL RULES?
YES _____   NO _____

IF YES, PLEASE EXPLAIN: _____

_____

_____

CAN I COUNT ON YOU TO BE AT YOUR JOB EVERY DAY FOR THE LENGTH OF THE TIME YOU ARE ASSIGNED?
YES _____   NO _____

QUALIFICATIONS: WHAT MAKES YOU RIGHT FOR THIS JOB? _____

_____

_____

REFERENCES: NAME AND COMMENT ON APPLICANT'S SINCERITY AND SKILLS
TEACHER: _____
TEACHER: _____
PARENT: _____
OTHER: _____

attention: Sneak in some personal time as students are hanging up coats, on the playground before school or during lunch, or during a free-choice time. Don't talk about school—key in on your students' likes and dislikes. Find each individual child's hook, whether it's wrestling, horseback riding, music, or another activity. Noting these can be invaluable when working toward rewards, and, more importantly, the children will know you are truly interested in them as individuals and not just as students.

▶ 2. If you think you can find absolutely nothing positive in a student, look harder. If you are not able to find something to like about every child, how can you expect children to see one another in a positive light? You teach tolerance and ask them to compliment their classmates—why should you be the exception? Remember, you may be the *only* person that connects with a child on a positive level—find something good in each student every day.

▶ 3. Despite your best efforts, you may still have disrespectful students in your classroom. If you have someone who is consistently rude to peers and adults, it could be helpful to do some investigating into the child's home situation. Extremely upsetting things might be happening that would account for the inappropriate behavior. Of course, this should not be an excuse for disruption and disrespect. If things continue to deteriorate, you may need to meet with other professionals in your building (for example, a psychologist, guidance counselor, and social worker) to develop strategies to address the problem. Don't forget to document your efforts, and reconvene your group if things are not working. Remember, it is not your sole responsibility to address these kinds of concerns.

▶ 4. Students who are chronically rude and disrespectful can truly try your patience. But remember to control your anger. Hindsight is 20/20, so be proactive and take the time to think and breathe. Chances are good you will be able to avoid a power struggle or frustrating screaming match. When particularly difficult students push your every button, remove them from the classroom until you are able to deal with them alone. If removal is impossible, take a minute to cool down, and put the problem temporarily aside to be addressed in private at a later time. A showdown in front of the entire class leaves the student (and possibly yourself) with little hope of saving face. Treat the difficult student as you would like to be treated under the circumstances. Make every attempt to discipline with dignity.

 If the student who is being disrespectful and rude is a special education student, be sure to consult with the special education teacher. Have a copy of the individual education plan (IEP), and look for a behavior goal and a behavior plan. Be aware of the 10-day limit for suspensions, and remember that if the student is given in-house suspensions, the IEP must be implemented during that time. Realize that you should be able to access the help of other special education support staff, in addition to the teacher, to help you address your concerns about the student.

Super Student of the Week

Do you shudder whenever you need to choose a monitor to send on an errand? If you end up with one smiling student and all the rest in various stages of moaning, sighing, groaning, and pouting, here's a super way to keep 'em all happy.

▶ 1. Instead of choosing different students to run any errands that may be necessary during your day, choose a Super Student of the Week (SSOTW) who is in charge of all monitoring jobs during a particular week. (For kindergartners and first graders, choose a Special Person instead of an SSOTW. See the paragraphs marked with light bulb icons for more about the Special Person.)

▶ 2. Number slips of paper corresponding to the number of students in your room, and drop the slips into a container. Choose one number at the end of your weekly classroom meeting every Friday. This student will be the Super Student of the Week beginning the following Monday.

▶ 3. Encourage the SSOTW to bring in and display any personal items that would be interesting to share with the class. It may be best to have the student bring the items on Friday, for one day only, to minimize the chance they could be lost, broken, or stolen. Be sure to provide a special place that is safe for these items. Perhaps a small table or a desk near your desk would work. At the end of the week, during your classroom meeting, the SSOTW is accorded 15 minutes of fame—a time to talk about herself or himself and the personal items being shared. It is helpful if you can be the person to share first to model for students who will do so in the future.

▶ 4. If you do not feel choosing an SSOTW is a practice you want to implement in your classroom, use your class roster to choose a new monitor for the week to run your errands. You can go down your list alphabetically to choose your helper each week, and announce to your class each Friday who that person will be for the following week. Make sure monitors understand your expectations for hallway travel and any other responsibilities you may assign. You'll never find yourself in the unpleasant position of hemming and hawing about whom to choose for a monitor again.

▶ 5. Note that it is usually better to select a helper each week than each day. It is much easier for you to keep track of your helper weekly than daily. Also, it provides an opportunity to gauge how responsible a student can be over a longer period of time. In this way, you will know who may need reminders about behavior the next time their turn comes around.

 Kindergarten and early primary teachers know that young children aren't as patient as their older counterparts in waiting for a turn to be special. Create a leader sign or pin for the daily monitor to wear. Then move down your class list daily to choose someone. Often, younger students travel in twos when doing jobs that take them out of the classroom. You may want to have your monitor of the day choose a partner, making sure that different students are selected each day. You could vary this procedure by choosing two students yourself or even having your previous day's monitors pick two names from a hat. When the hat is empty, start all over again.

Kindergarten and early primary children benefit greatly from your providing a time each week to highlight a Special Person (instead of an SSOTW). This helps them to see how their interests and families are like those of their peers as well as how they are different. The following is one way you may choose to do this.

▶ 1. Draw names or select another way to decide on the Special Person, and have classmates help you determine one or two privileges for that child, such as being monitor or messenger.

▶ 2. Provide bulletin board space or another area for a child to display special items, such as favorite toys, books, pictures, and special interests.

▶ 3. Provide each child with a prepared family book at the beginning of the school year, to be filled in at home with photographs, the child's drawings, and magazine pictures. Books come back to school and are placed in a special container to be read throughout the year by other students. This book is part of the Special Person's display and will be read to the class by the teacher, child, or parent during Special Person sharing time. A family book includes a page each with the following information and room for the aforementioned items.

   a. _____'s Family Book by_____ (cover)

   b. This is my family.

   c. This is my home. My address is_____. My telephone number is_____.

   d. My family likes to celebrate . . .

   e. My family has fun when we . . .

   f. My family works together when we . . .

   g. My family likes to eat . . .

   h. These are the countries of my ancestors:

   i. Did you like this book? Yes___ No___

▶ 4. Arrange a convenient time for parents, grandparents, and siblings to visit the classroom and be introduced to the class. Encourage parents to share foods, clothing, and items unique to their culture or to share special hobbies or family activities.

▶ 5. Have each child make a Me Mobile (Figure 2.3) at the beginning of the year. On five differently shaped cardboard squares hanging down, the children can tell about themselves with a self-portrait, two favorite colors,

Figure 2.3 The Me Mobile

first and last name, something they are good at, and two favorite classroom activities. Hang these mobiles to emphasize who lives in your classroom, and be sure to use it at Special Person sharing time.

Classroom Meetings

Sharing time can be a nurturing and illuminating opportunity for classroom families as well as biological families. Here's an organized way to make that happen.

▶ 1. Make holding a classroom meeting a weekly tradition. Set aside about one-half hour a week—Fridays are a good choice—and spend time debriefing students about the week's experiences. During the first few meetings, be sure to clearly explain your expectations. Guidelines can include the following.

    a. Raise your hand to speak.

    b. Listen politely while another person is talking to you, and don't repeat what someone else has said.

    c. Tattling and complaining are not allowed.

    d. Be supportive of what others have to say.

▶ 2. It is critical for you to facilitate and guide each meeting to keep the discussion productive. Without structure and your guidance, meetings can deteriorate and lose value and effectiveness.

▶ 3. To help provide some open discussion for the meeting, place a box or hang a large envelope somewhere in the room where students can put written suggestions and concerns. These can include ideas for field trips, classroom activities, treats, and so on. Students should also know your rules about when they may take the time to write and place these suggestions in the box or envelope. You may also want to offer children the chance to tell you something privately this way. Be sure to tell your students to indicate on their message that it is not to be shared during the classroom meeting.

▶ 4. Prepare a chart to use at each meeting that will assist in moving the students through the process. For example:

    a. What did you like about school this week?

    b. What didn't you like?

    c. What is something good that happened to you in school this week?

    d. Is there anything with which you need help or that you would like to talk about?

▶ 5. Open discussion can follow. This is an opportunity to share things students have written and placed in the special box or envelope. It is also time for you to share compliments, air concerns, discuss upcoming events, and, finally, distribute the newsletter to students to take home. Keep the discussion going, and take students' suggestions and comments seriously. This is your time to listen and to learn what is working in your classroom and what is not. Then *you* decide whether changes or modifications are possible. The meeting ends with the Super Student of the Week sharing personal items and her or his family book with the class. (See #3 under Super Student of the Week on page 19.)

Compliment Book

Are your students befuddled by your kind words? Freaked out by your flattery? Awestruck by your approval? Help them deal with your plethora of praise by teaching the lost art of the sincere compliment.

▶ 1. Take some time in your classroom to talk about compliments—the sincere kind. Differentiate between a false compliment and a sincere one. Let your students practice giving compliments to you and to one another. This skill is often lost or forgotten, and children of all ages need to practice sincere kindness to others.

▶ 2. Every Friday before the classroom meeting, have your students spend time writing a compliment for the Super Student of the Week. Provide an open-ended stem such as

Dear _____,

I am glad you were the Super Student of the Week because

_____

Your friend,

_____

This is also an excellent way to review friendly letter-writing on a weekly basis, and students look forward to writing the compliments as much as they do receiving them when it's their turn. While students are writing, circulate among them helping proofread. Don't forget to compliment *their* good work.

▶ 3. A drawing is also done to go along with the student's compliment—even older children enjoy adding this touch. An easy way to include drawing and the written compliment is to use half lined and half blank primary paper. For older students, you may want to just use a notebook size piece of lined paper for both the message and the picture. For younger children, have them write a compliment about, and draw a picture of, the Special Person (instead of an SSOTW).

▶ 4. The Super Student of the Week designs a cover for the compliment book and can't wait to take it home on Friday.

Wall of Fame

Do you have to harass students to turn in homework? Are the numbers of absences you're recording absolutely absurd? Here's a way to motivate and praise those who complete all assignments and are in school every day.

▶ 1. Designate an area in your classroom to display a Wall of Fame—a brick-patterned bulletin board or wall area large enough to hold stars equal to the number of students in your class. You can cut bricks out of construction paper or use a rectangular sponge dipped in paint to print brick shapes for your wall. Laminating the finished product will ensure its use again next year. (Are you artistically challenged—even when it comes to drawing bricks? Keep your eyes open around Christmas for stores selling decorations or supplies, and you'll find brick paper that will work just fine.)

▶ 2. Give each child a star made from stiff paper or card stock during the first days of school to decorate with their name and a design of their choice. Laminate these stars, as they will be used all year long. Then, explain to your students that if they have perfect attendance and complete all work for an entire week, their star will be displayed on the Wall of Fame.

▶ 3. Every Monday morning, take time to announce Wall of Fame students from the previous week. Stars of students who were absent or did not complete work are removed, new stars may go up, and some may remain. Be sure to recognize Wall of Famers in your weekly newsletter—children love seeing their names in print for something special.

► 4. At the end of the first semester, and then again at the close of second semester, you may want to award certificates to students who made an outstanding effort to remain on the Wall of Fame. You decide how many weeks that should be. You may also want to have total year rewards and even give an extra bonus—book, game, special time with you—to the student who has had the highest number of weeks on the Wall during the school year.

Figure 2.4 Wall of Fame

Tattling

Tattling can be just like the flu—it's catching and can reach epidemic proportions in your classroom. There is no miracle cure, but these ideas may help curb the spread.

▶ 1. You will want to discuss this unpleasant habit as part of the effort to create a family atmosphere in your classroom. It may help to clarify in your students' minds the kind of information you want to hear from them and the kind you don't. Explain the difference between a report and a tattle. A *report* alerts the teacher to something that could be harmful to someone or something at school. A *tattle* is telling about someone to get that person in trouble. You may want to give some examples, and ask your students to give some so you have a sense that they know the difference.

▶ 2. When students come to you—and they will—to tattle, review briefly the difference between a report and a tattle. Even younger children can begin to understand that they are not the same. Frequent reminders to the entire class as well as discouraging students who are clearly coming to you with a tattle are ways to begin to squelch this bad habit.

▶ 3. Be advised this can be a difficult habit to break. If you have students who just can't seem to stop, here are some ways to redirect the tattling.

     a. Draw a huge ear, and mount it on a wall or bulletin board at student height. (Not an artist? Find a picture, and enlarge it using your overhead projector.) Tell the children that if they must tattle, whisper it to the giant ear. Some children may use it for a while, but it will probably provide the cure, especially for older students.

     b. Provide a box or envelope and mark it "For Tattles." Encourage students to write their tattles and place them inside. Let them know, however, that you will not read these. This, of course, will be discouraging for any student who thinks it will provide a silent pipeline to you.

▶ 4. It's very important to emphasize to your class that you do want to know important things—matters that could be serious. This is especially significant for younger children who may feel shy, afraid, or confused about what they should tell you. Let your students know that if they're confused about something they want to tell you and really don't know if it's a tattle or a report, then they should tell you. Encourage them to say they are confused and need your help. It's better to err on the side of allowing a tattle than to ignore a potentially serious situation.

3

Working With Diverse Student and Family Populations

Schools today reflect our changing society, which is becoming more culturally and socioeconomically diverse. We have students in our classrooms who come from a variety of backgrounds. We must work with families who do not speak English or who may be illiterate. Most school districts have resources to help in this regard, so be sure to check with yours. Here are some additional suggestions as to how you can meet this challenge in your own classroom.

Chapter Outline

- Working With Non-English-Speaking Students
- Making Non-English-Speaking Students Comfortable in Your Classroom
- Working With Non-English-Speaking Families
- Working With Family Members Who May Be Illiterate

Working With Non-English-Speaking Students

Do you find yourself listening with envy to colleagues or friends who are fluent in a foreign language? If only you had taken a language in high school. This could be very helpful, but there are other things you can do to help a non-English-speaking student be successful in your classroom. Here are some ideas.

▶ 1. The first thing to do is to familiarize yourself with what your school district has to offer in the area of assistance for teachers with non-English-speaking students in their classrooms. It's a good idea to do this before you have a student for whom you will require this kind of help. Most districts have a bilingual department that can connect teachers with someone who can assist them. You need to be especially concerned about communicating with parents, and your school or school district should provide you with someone who can talk to parents in their native language.

▶ 2. If a student who does not speak English is placed in your classroom, you may want to see if anyone in your class is bilingual and can translate for that student. If you don't have anyone in your room, perhaps a colleague will have a student who can assist. If there is no student, maybe another teacher or a paraprofessional can help in some way. If the student receives special education services, be sure to work closely with the special education teacher to provide the scope of services necessary.

▶ 3. Be sure to observe the non-English-speaking student's progress—emotionally and socially as well as academically. If necessary, document concerns you have, and collect work samples or evidence of lack of progress. Some parents want their children immersed in an English-speaking atmosphere, feeling it will be the best way for them to learn the language. This may not work for all children, and you need to be aware if you think this may be happening. Be sure you keep your principal informed if you suspect the child is having significant difficulties. The principal should then be able to arrange to meet with you, the parents, and someone from the bilingual department to discuss concerns regarding the child's progress.

▶ 4. Be sure to arrange for someone to translate during parent conferences. There may be a sibling or another family member who speaks English who can assist. Otherwise, another staff member or paraprofessional may be available to help. If you are unable to find anyone, let your principal know. The principal may arrange something or tell you to contact someone from the bilingual department in your district. Note that you should make plans well in advance to ensure the availability of someone to translate for you.

Making Non-English-Speaking Students Comfortable in Your Classroom

Does a feeling of inadequacy rear its ugly head as you think about how you will make your new non-English-speaking student comfortable in your very American classroom? Along with smiles, kindness, consideration, and helpfulness from both you and your students, here are a few additional suggestions to try.

▶ 1. Warm smiles are a universal sign of friendship. Be sure there of plenty of them from you and your students. Make an effort to see that the new student is included in all of your classroom activities. Be sure to seat the non-English-speaking student near a mature and helpful classmate. See that the new student has a responsible buddy who can help in the lunch line, in special classes, and anywhere else you think assistance may be needed. Encourage your students to include their classmate in games and activities on the playground during recess.

▶ 2. As noted previously, make an effort to see if someone—either another student or adult in your school—can assist occasionally in translating, especially in the beginning. You may want to learn a few critical words and phrases in the child's native language, such as *bathroom, lunch, do you understand, are you OK,* and so on. This can help smooth the way in some potential crisis situations. In turn, help the student to learn some words and phrases that will help her or him to communicate with you in urgent situations—you can decide what would be most important in your own classroom and school environment.

▶ 3. Make family contact immediately, and find out what the situation is regarding someone who can speak English. If possible, use that person as your contact, and get a phone number. If there is no one in the family who speaks English, find someone you can count on to translate for you— either in your school or from your district's bilingual department.

▶ 4. Plan to spend some social studies time learning about the new student's native country. Invite family members in to share customs, food, and information about their country. Display information, pictures, artifacts, and so on from the student's homeland. Also introduce your new class member to some typically American things—foods, games, famous people and places, and so forth. What an opportunity for some wonderful cultural exchange and a great learning experience for everybody!

Working With Non-English-Speaking Families

Do you feel overwhelmed with the prospect of trying to communicate with families who don't speak English? As more non-English-speaking children enter our schools, we are challenged with the additional task of helping these parents be our partners in educating their children. Help is on the way from parent advocate groups, community groups, and your own school district. Here are some other ideas you can use right away.

▶ 1. As noted previously, it is imperative that you make contact as soon as possible with family members of your non-English-speaking students. Try to find out if anyone at home speaks English and if you can use that person as your contact for emergencies as well as for general communication. If no family member speaks English, talk to your principal about how to arrange for someone to translate and also about what the procedure will be in an emergency situation—especially if there is no one in the building who speaks the child's native language.

▶ 2. Be aware of how the bilingual department in your school district operates. Get the names and phone numbers of people who can help translate the languages students in your classroom speak. Perhaps they can help you learn some critical words and phrases when you need to contact parents quickly. These might include "This is Ms. Blank. Please call Maple School as soon as possible. The number is _____" or "Tran is ill. Please call Maple School at _____." You get the idea—decide what would be most helpful for you to know.

▶ 3. Do your best to get family members to attend parent conferences. Again, you may need to have someone translate your phone call or even the letter of invitation you send to the parents. It is your job to see that this information gets to the families in some form. Don't forget to make arrangements for a translator during the conference. Perhaps someone at your school can help, or contact the bilingual department. In many cities, there are various ethnic community organizations that will support non-English-speaking parents by acting as translators and even bring the parents to their meeting with you. Remember, however, to give them notice well in advance so you don't find yourself with no way to communicate with parents who have come to talk with you.

▶ 4. Contact with all parents on a regular basis is very important, and non-English-speaking parents must be included. If no one is around to translate and help you to make occasional phone calls when needed, a letter home once a month may work. This would give you enough time to write your letter and have someone translate it. A monthly letter helps keep the parents abreast of your classroom activities and can also act as a mini report card for the student. Then, when parent conference time rolls around, the family already has some up-to-date background information.

Working With Family Members Who May Be Illiterate

Working with family members who you think may be illiterate can be a delicate issue and one you may feel uncomfortable addressing. This is another challenge— but one you can meet. Just remember, most parents want the best for their children and will work with you to ensure success for them. Read on for some ways to meet this challenge with sensitivity.

▶ 1. "How do I know if family members can't read?" you ask. Do you send notes and permission slips home that are never returned? Don't assume parents aren't interested—there may be another reason. Do a little investigating with your student. Ask about the items that you send home and about why they are never returned. If the student is evasive or has an implausible answer each time you ask, consider the possibility that no one at home can read. Your student shouldn't miss out on school activities because there is no one who can read your notes.

▶ 2. Be careful, however, that you have investigated all possibilities before you decide there may be a literacy problem. Are the notes getting home with your student? Is the student afraid the notes are bad reports and destroying or hiding them? Take time in class to go over your communications so your class knows exactly what is being sent home. Some teachers only report problems or concerns over the phone, to avoid the fear some students have of "bad notes" being sent home. Contact parents by phone if you suspect the student may not be taking things home. This simple action could clear up the problem.

▶ 3. However, if you have come to the conclusion that there may be a literacy problem, you need to think of ways you can get information home in a timely manner so that the student can participate in classroom or school events. When students are fourth graders or beyond, you may be able to meet with them whenever something needs to go home to read it over and indicate what type of response, if any, is needed from the parent. You may need to come right out and say you are concerned that the parent can't read the important notes you send home and that you need the student's help. If your student is younger or unreliable, try to find out if there is an older sibling in school. If there is, schedule a time to meet discreetly with the sibling on a weekly basis to go over written communications that will be going home. Ask the sibling to be sure the parent knows the contents of the note and signs or responds appropriately. Here, also, you may need to be frank and say you are concerned that the parent can't read and that you need the sibling's assistance.

▶ 4. Depending on your comfort level with the parents or family members, you may be able to broach the issue with them directly. You might say something like, "I noticed the notes I'm sending home aren't being returned. May I ask if you are unable to read them?" It may be a great relief to the family members to finally be able to deal with the issue honestly. Then the lines of communication are open, and arrangements can be made to ensure that your notes are addressed.

▶ 5. If you are uncomfortable with the idea of calling family members, talk to another building professional such as the school social worker, who has extensive experience working with people of diverse socioeconomic backgrounds and should be able to assist you with this issue. You may also want to talk this over with your principal if you are particularly concerned about a specific family circumstance. Whatever the case, don't ignore this situation at the risk of denying your student access to school and classroom events.

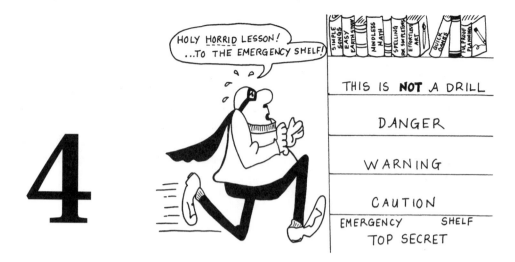

With-it-ness

With-it-ness—that strange word familiar to all educators—describes a most important quality necessary for good teachers to develop. When you have mastered it, your students wonder if you have eyes in the back of your head—and you can answer, almost truthfully, "Yes!" This takes time; however, you can begin adding one or two strategies to your teaching repertoire right away and add more as you become more experienced. With-it-ness is one of the most valuable tools any teacher can have.

Chapter Outline

- Teacher Behavior
- Planning Ahead and Lesson Expectations
- If a Lesson Really Isn't Working
- Looks, Gestures, Posture, and Positioning in Room to Convey Expectations
- Demeanor and Actions During Lessons to Ensure Student Focus
- Modeling Expected Responses
- The Challenging Student

A number of necessary and very useful teacher behaviors are a must for your repertoire. Here are a few of the most valuable—they're helpful no matter what you're doing in your classroom.

Teacher Behavior

▶ 1. A key tool for any teacher is with-it-ness, the ability to be consistently aware of what is happening in the classroom. The best way to do this is to have expectations for *every* activity that goes on. You must know in your mind exactly what you want the activity to look like, and you must impart those expectations to your students.

  a. *Example One.* You may decide that your math lesson looks like this. All students' desks are clear except for their math books as you explain the lesson and ask for student interaction. This allows you to scan the room to see exactly who you can compliment and who needs redirection. You continue to scan with this expectation in mind as you teach the lesson. You stop anytime you see someone not following your instructions.

  b. *Example Two.* You decide your classroom line should look like this. Each child should be in an assigned place in line, looking forward. Arms are folded in front, and there is no talking. Students know that the line will not move until everyone complies. These expectations allow you to scan the line to see who you can compliment and who needs redirection. You continue to do so as your line moves through the hallway.

▶ 2. Shaping students' actions—either academically or behaviorally—will be done through *your* actions and words, and it can be done in a positive way.

  a. *Give directions only when you have the attention of all your students.* Scan the room to be sure all eyes are on you. Make sure the directions are simple and specific. You may want to ask one or two students to repeat them. Expect that students will wait to comply until you have given the signal. Be quick to praise those individuals or groups of students who respond immediately.

  b. *Move around your classroom as you teach.* Standing or sitting in one place limits your ability to monitor your students' attention or lack thereof. If your students know you always circulate as you teach, they will be less inclined to be inattentive and off task.

  c. *Always take the time as you teach to compliment, compliment, compliment those in class who are attentive and following directions.* This greatly improves the chances of off-task students complying also.

  d. *Follow through on anything you say you will do—whether positive or negative.* Trust is built when children know you are as good as your word. So be careful with the promises you make.

  e. *Nothing is more important than keeping your students attentive and focused during the school day.* Your lesson, no matter how well prepared, will not be successful if students are not engaged. Remember to repeat your expectations, compliment focused students, and use individual and group reward systems to maintain the control that will ensure that learning is happening in your classroom.

f. *As you monitor students who are working or listening, compliment specific behavior you are looking for, as a way to model it for other students.* For example: "Trenay, I really like the way you are listing ways to solve this problem on your paper and remembering to number each one. I notice the only things on your desk are your science book, paper, and pencil. Thank you for following my directions."

g. *Rules in your classroom are not made to be broken.* You greatly minimize the effectiveness of your rules if you are constantly making exceptions. So put some real thought into making them. For example: In deciding when pencils will be sharpened, you may choose first thing in the morning and again first thing in the afternoon, being sure each student sharpens more than one pencil.

Then consider Murphy's Law—anything that can go wrong, will go wrong. You need to think of how or why some student will inevitably be without a sharp pencil and how you will solve the problem. Remember, Murphy's Law applies to every rule you have in your classroom.

Planning Ahead and Lesson Expectations

Are you afflicted with stage fright whenever you teach a lesson? Do you break out in a cold sweat when you misplace your book or drop your chalk? Try implementing these helpful ideas to calm your frazzled nerves.

▶ 1. Don't plan to teach a lesson you have not thought out thoroughly. Unplanned or poorly planned lessons are seldom successful. Be sure you create a step-by-step procedure—an in-depth extension of your lesson plan book. You may even want to list important points or concepts on index cards as a reference for yourself during the lesson. Make a list of all the materials you will need both for yourself and for your students.

▶ 2. Mentally rehearse the lesson. This includes invoking Murphy's Law once again. As you think about the lesson, consider where there could be glitches. For example, you plan to have students use books to research a certain topic. Will they work individually or in groups? Will there be enough books for everyone? Will the books actually contain the information for which they are searching? Do your students know how to use a table of contents, an index, headings within chapters?

▶ 3. Be sure all the materials you will need for yourself and your students are close at hand and in the order in which you will need them. Count to be sure you have the right number of worksheets, scissors, glue bottles, and so forth. Do this well in advance—don't wait until it's too late to make more copies, borrow three scissors, or fill those empty glue bottles.

▶ 4. Tell the class your plans for the lesson. Don't let every step be a surprise. Give them the big picture and then the smaller steps they will take to complete the task. This will avoid ongoing questions—such as "What are those green Ping-Pong balls for?"—and allow students to settle down to the tasks you have planned. Also remember to allow for the teachable moment. Consider the possibility that your lesson may take a valuable detour. Relax and use the opportunity. As a result, you may find you want to add a new dimension to tomorrow's presentation.

▶ 5. Conclude the lesson before boredom sets in—even if it means you must cut it short. Once students' attention significantly begins to wander, learning has ceased. At this point, you should already be thinking about changes and improvements for tomorrow's lesson. Spend time reflecting on what was going on when you lost them. Your students will experience greater success when you become your own toughest critic.

Consider your special education students when planning your lesson. If you are fortunate enough to have a special education teacher in your classroom during some lessons, be sure to share your lesson plans with this colleague, who will be able to provide modifications and assistance to the special education students during the lesson. Planning to meet regularly with this special education teacher will also ensure that you are both on the same page for your daily lessons. If you are alone, consult with the special education teacher to get some ideas as to how you can best assist the student during the lesson. You may want to seat the student next to someone who can assist. If small group activities are involved, be sure special education students have an assignment in the group at which they can be successful. If information needs to be copied during a lesson, you may want to provide these students with a copy of the material when the lesson is completed, to be sure they are up-to-date.

If a Lesson Really Isn't Working

You're well into a lesson when you realize that it never really got off the ground. Questioning looks appear on some little faces while others reacquaint themselves with the messes inside their desks or the fly buzzing around the room—well, you get the idea. If calling 911 isn't an option for you—try this.

▶ 1. Remember, the best laid plans will fail sometimes. The causes could be anything—you may have assumed students already had absorbed and understood information needed for the current lesson, your well-planned explanation doesn't seem to be making sense to your students, or there's a full moon. Whatever the reason, your lesson has failed.

► 2. You need a contingency plan. Have an emergency shelf somewhere in the room that houses an extra, all-purpose art project that can be used anytime during the year, or a story to read, or a quick and easy writing lesson—so you don't find yourself with 45 minutes and nothing to do. Be sure, however, that you have gathered all the needed supplies for your emergency lesson. You want to make as smooth a transition as possible from your troubled lesson to one you know will go smoothly and has every chance of success. (Don't forget to restock your emergency shelf once you have used the materials.)

► 3. Remember—don't beat a lesson to death. If you can think quickly on your feet and rescue the lesson by doing things another way on the spot, great. If not, simply stop, and use your emergency materials. Tomorrow is another day—give yourself a chance to regroup and approach the lesson from a different perspective.

► 4. When you rethink your lesson, take time to analyze what went wrong. If it wasn't a full moon, then you may need to teach some information critical to the new lesson or reteach something you thought your students already knew. If you simply present the same lesson again, you run the risk of similar disappointing results.

Transitioning is extremely important for young children when a lesson is not going well.

► 1. Never continue a directed or an independent activity when children are noisy or are confused as to what to do.

► 2. Stop and gain their attention by reminding them about the steps in active listening.

► 3. Model the directions again using one or two children who were listening or who understood and followed the directions the first time.

► 4. It may be necessary to clear desks or tables of unnecessary materials that could cause distractions.

► 5. When you have the attention of all the children, begin again.

These techniques work all through the year. You will find, however, that the children's attention span grows as the year progresses, and so the time that they are able to focus on an activity lengthens. Early in the year, kindergarten and first-grade students are more successful if work periods and discussion times are about 15 to 20 minutes in length. The goal is to gradually lengthen their attention span.

Steps in active listening for young children can be verbalized in the following way.

a. I am looking for quiet bodies and hands.
b. I am looking for quiet mouths.

c. I am looking to see if everyone's eyes are on me.

You could also provide this information in an interactive way such as a song or rap, which is a very effective way to draw young children in and redirect their attention. You could use a familiar tune and make up your own simple words to use each time you need to refocus your group.

Looks, Gestures, Posture, and Positioning in Room to Convey Expectations

If your bag of teaching tricks is full of meaningful looks, gestures, and postures that reinforce what you say to students—then you understand that what you do is as important as what you say while you teach.

▶ 1. Your facial expression can convey a great deal to your students—even from across the room. For example, raised eyebrows can say "Are you paying attention?" or "What are you doing?" or "Are you following my directions?" A nod of your head can encourage an unsure student to go on with an answer or can indicate "That's right" or "Yes, you may go to the bathroom." A slight frown can mean "I'm not pleased with what I am seeing," or "Please stop and pay attention," or even "Are you confused?" You can convey many unspoken messages to your students with facial expressions. They allow you to continue with your lessons while making an additional point to a group of students or an individual. Develop some for your repertoire.

▶ 2. Many teachers use gestures as signals for their students. A raised hand can mean "Put your hands up if you are listening and ready to follow my directions." Thumbs up or down can mean "Indicate whether you agree or not." Gestures can simply mean what they indicate—"Please move," "Go to the back of the line," or "Turn around." They, too, can be a very valuable asset to your teaching repertoire that will allow you to teach while sending different nonverbal messages at the same time.

▶ 3. Moving around the room while teaching is probably one of the most important things a teacher can do. If your students know you circulate whenever you can as you teach, they will be far more likely to stay focused and on task—especially those with a tendency to let their eyes wander, to play, or to daydream. You may be surprised how many problems—both academic and behavioral—you can minimize or prevent if you make it a habit to move around the room and watch your students work. Proximity control fits here also. Standing near a noncompliant student usually sends a message that you are aware of what is going on, and this alone will often refocus the student.

▶ 4. Never underestimate the value and importance of eye contact. Catching a student's eye can send a positive message or one of concern. Add a smile when an on-task or well-behaved student returns your glance, and you've paid a compliment. Add raised eyebrows or a frown, and you've sent a warning to someone teetering on the brink of a problem. Eye contact with your students while you are teaching a lesson tells them you are aware of all that is going on and are alert for both good and bad behavior as well as for children who are working and those who are not. Eye contact while complimenting a student says, "I sincerely mean what I say." When you make someone aware of negative consequences while making eye contact, you imply, "Take me seriously; I mean it, and I will follow through."

Demeanor and Actions During Lessons to Ensure Student Focus

Do you wonder if your students are listening to someone behind you giving an entirely different set of directions or teaching a lesson totally unlike the one you are teaching? If no one is there, could the problem be yours?

▶   1. If you want your students to respond in a certain way when you give directions or teach a lesson, then you need to set expectations and be sure they are understood. Also, it is very important to be consistent with whatever expectations you set.

▶   2. Develop a technique to get your students' attention, and use it every time you want them to focus on you. (For an easy-to-use idea, see Chapter 5 under the heading One Subject to Another on page 42.) Eventually, your students will know what to expect and how to respond. A great deal of time will be saved.

▶   3. Be sure you make a habit of reminding students to wait to comply until after you have completed giving all your directions. Compliment those who adhere immediately. Stop giving directions if even one person is not listening or is going ahead.

▶   4. Be sure your students know what you expect of them when you are talking. You should expect clear desks (or only needed supplies), hands where you can see them, and all eyes on you. Your entire class should know that there are no exceptions and that you will not go on with the lesson if even one student is noncompliant.

▶   5. Be sure to use eye contact, facial expression, proximity control, and movement to emphasize the ideas listed above. These things, combined with your verbal directions, should set very clear expectations for your students. If you are consistent in using them, they become time-savers as well.

Modeling Expected Responses

If you think you must be from Mars—or your students are—when you give clear directions that no one seems to understand, remember that old Martian saying: One picture is worth 1,000 words.

▶ 1. When giving directions, remember that what seems to come out of your mouth clearly and simply does not necessarily enter the ears of your students that way. Experience has taught many teachers that they must anticipate confusion when giving directions and that often demonstrating the expected response can save time and frustration for both teacher and students.

▶ 2. Keep directions simple with only a few steps—especially at the beginning of the year, even with older students. If the directions, of necessity, must be more complex, provide only a part of them at a time. When everyone has complied, continue.

▶ 3. The key is to demonstrate what you want, especially at first. You must assume that your directions will confuse at least some of your students. For this reason, repetition and demonstration are very important. As your class becomes accustomed to your expectations, this will, of course, become less and less necessary. Sometimes, as the year wears on, you will need to refresh memories again. Don't hesitate to do this, or you may be faced with deteriorating responses to your expectations.

▶ 4. For some lessons, you can demonstrate what you desire from your class. At other times, let one or two students do it for you. Ask someone to raise a hand and show the class, for example, how a desk should look when a student is ready for math—only one sheet of paper, a pencil, and a math book on the desk. It is important to reiterate these expectations as students prepare for the lesson. Praise those who comply, and do not begin until everyone has done so.

▶ 5. If you are teaching a lesson requiring students to respond in a step-by-step manner, show only one or two steps (depending on how complex they are) at a time. When finished, the students are to wait for further directions. Again, praise those students who comply, and also verbally explain their compliance. For example, "I am happy to see Monique has cut out two orange pumpkins and drawn a different face on each one. She has decided where she will place them on her black paper, and now she is waiting for further directions. Excellent." Do not continue until everyone has gotten to that point. Be sure to circulate to see that no one has made a mistake or gone ahead. You can do the same with simple directions, such as raising hands to speak. If someone talks out, simply raise your hand—children usually catch on quickly and will imitate you. If someone stands up to speak to you, you may want to compliment a student who responded correctly and say, "I see LaTasha's hand is raised to ask a question. I'll be right over to answer it. Thank you for staying seated and raising your hand."

The Challenging Student

You've tried all the strategies in this chapter. They're simple, effective, and work with most of the students in your classroom. But how do you handle those few who just won't comply no matter what you do? First, accept the fact that THE PERFECT CLASSROOM doesn't exist. Then try this.

▶ 1. Most teachers can identify challenging students early in the school year. Once you know who they are, be scientific in planning your strategies to keep their disturbing behavior to a minimum. Ask yourself the following questions.

    a. Where can I seat the student to be surrounded by positive role models?

    b. How can I position the student in line to be surrounded by positive role models?

    c. How can I anticipate problems in special classes and coordinate a system of rewards and negative consequences with those teachers and the students involved?

    d. Can I enlist the help of family members in positive ways to improve the student's behavior?

▶ 2. Once you have done the aforementioned planning, consider the following ideas as you think about your daily activities and how you can minimize the effects of challenging students. Here are just a few suggestions.

    a. When you are moving students within your classroom, try moving the disruptive students first. If they still disturb others, consider having them stay with you until everyone else has moved; then allow them to take their assigned positions.

    b. When you are moving your class outside your room, realize that as a whole, they will probably never be perfectly still and silent as they wait to go. Problem students inevitably choose these times to create trouble. Catch the whole group when they are—in your mind—most ready to go, and move them immediately. (If you wait too long, you risk disruption.) Compliment and praise the group and individuals who behave appropriately—especially praise the difficult students if they are behaving.

    c. Be careful not to set up the challenging students—in other words, do your best to keep from placing them in situations where they will surely find trouble. For example, you may want to allow such students to run errands at some point, and sending along another trustworthy person may help prevent hallway misbehavior.

    d. Watch like a hawk for appropriate behavior on the part of the challenging students—catch them being good. Sincerely compliment them whenever you can. Small, tangible or edible rewards, if they are permitted in your school, can occasionally be given.

    e. Enlist other students to catch the target student behaving appropriately. Verbal praise in front of the whole class or one-on-one can be effective. Other reward systems involving classmates can be set up to encourage appropriate behavior.

    f. Get in the habit of informing the student's family, by note or phone call, if the student has had a good day. This will encourage the appropriate behavior, the family's help with coordinating information on behavior at home, rewards at home for good school behavior, and negative consequences at home for inappropriate school behavior.

▶ 3. Realize that if you have tried all of these things, and certain students continue to seriously disrupt your class—if they consistently keep you from teaching and other children from learning—you may need to seek help from your principal as well as other professionals in the building. Don't hesitate to do this. You are not a bad teacher because you can't handle every child successfully yourself. Any veteran educator who is honest will agree.

If one of your challenging students is also a special education student, you should be sure to get a copy of the individual education plan (IEP) as soon as possible. This will allow you to understand the needs, both academic and behavioral, of the student. Consult with the special education teacher on a regular basis to help implement suggested strategies and to dialogue about the success of your efforts. Don't be afraid to ask the special education teacher to spend additional time in your classroom to observe the student and then to discuss ways to best assist the student either behaviorally or academically.

5

Transitioning

Of all the times during a school day that can shake a teacher's self-confidence, transitioning can be one of the worst—unless you have plans that you consistently implement. The word *structure* was never more applicable than when moving your students within or outside of the classroom. Successful transitioning can set the tone for whatever lesson follows. Chaos during these times can spill over and cause problems throughout your school day. Use some of these strategies to overcome your concerns about this critical time.

Chapter Outline

- One Subject to Another

- One Subject to Another: Moving Within the Room

- Moving for Group Learning Activities

- One Classroom to Another

One Subject to Another

Does transitioning from one subject to another leave you weary, hoarse, and frustrated? If your classroom structure seems to fall apart between lessons, remember that the best-laid plans need explanation, expectations, repetition, and reinforcement.

▶ 1. Your strategy for transitioning from one subject to another should be basically the same no matter what the subject. Explain the procedure to your students during the first days of school so that everyone is clear about what is expected.

▶ 2. One method that can be very effective is to count backwards from five to one, including a direction with each number. For example:

Five. You should be seated quietly by now.

Four. All your work should be in your desk by now.

Three. Your mouths should be closed by now.

Two. Your hands should be folded by now.

One. Your eyes should be on me by now.

If this litany is repeated often enough, children will soon know exactly what to do when you say only the numbers. Praise, of course, should be given to those who respond immediately. Once you have everyone's attention, you can give clear, specific directions for the next task. Compliment, or even provide small, tangible rewards, such as stickers, for those who transition smoothly.

▶ 3. Another technique, which can be effective also, involves using the same basic directions no matter what the subject. Begin the transition by providing a reminder: "You have 2 minutes to complete your thought, and then we will be ready to move on to math." Praise as you see students finishing. Be specific when it's time to stop: "Two minutes are up, and everyone should be putting away their journals now." Praise those who are complying. Then instruct students to listen and proceed only when you tell them to: "I want you to have your math book, one sheet of paper, and a pencil on your desk. I will know you are ready when your eyes are on me. Please get ready now." Stop immediately if you see someone moving before being told, and remind students they are not to move until instructed. Compliment students who adhere.

▶ 4. When using the technique in number three, it is very important not to move to the next step until *everyone* has complied with the current direction. Draw in students who are not following by praising others around them or by noting that you will wait to move on until everyone is ready. You may want to use proximity control and eye contact to indicate the student to whom you are referring.

▶ 5. You can combine the techniques in steps two and three by using the counting method and then giving directions for needed materials, as in step three. Be sure you do not go to another step until everyone has complied with the current one.

Successful transitioning for kindergarten and early primary children means that a teacher can move them from place to place within and outside the classroom and from one subject to another with a minimum of noise, disruption, and loss of learning time. There are several ways to do this.

▶ 1. One of the most natural ways occurs when there is a commonality between two subjects. For example, a science lesson discussing the habits of bears in winter can evolve into a math lesson with students patterning (season of hibernation, season of activity), counting (the days and months of hibernation), and adding or subtracting (the days of sleep and of hibernation in the context of a full year).

▶ 2. Use a gimmick such as a prop, costume, or book that grabs the children's attention and serves as a lead-in to the next subject. For example: Be very dramatic about putting on an insect T-shirt or an insect hat or letting children put a paper or plastic bug in a bug net if they can tell something they know about insects. Or use poems, songs, exercises, singing games, movement, or a dramatization of the next subject to provide not only a lead-in but also a change of pace that allows children to eliminate the restlessness that built up in the previous activity, so they can concentrate again.

▶ 3. Music helps move children from place to place and from activity to activity. It also helps them review facts from the previous day's lesson in a fun way, such as a rap, pattern, or chant. Because rap, clapping rhythms, and songs can hold lots of information, facts learned through music are retained more easily and longer. Here is a sample of a chant: "Give us a fact! Give us a fact! Give us a fact, fact, fact!" When a child states a fact, add it to the chant, and go on asking for more. Do this quickly, add hand claps, foot stomps, and, again, children release energy built up from sitting. Then they can move on to a new lesson confidant of their background knowledge.

▶ 4. Take a recess break either outside or in a spacious breakout area where large muscle movements allow children the exercise needed to return to the quiet concentration of an academic lesson.

▶ 5. Provide a routine for getting work materials to the class through cubbies, work stations, table work tubs, or monitors—to ensure a calm, orderly change from one activity to another.

One Subject to Another: Moving Within the Room

Does stampede mentality take over once again when it's time for students to move to reading, math, or other large groups within your classroom? Here's a way to eliminate some of your stress and help ensure a quiet and orderly start to the lesson.

▶ 1. Before you begin, be sure you have two things in place. First, be clear yourself about exactly how you plan to move students into groups. Then, be sure you have the attention of the entire class—desks cleared except for needed supplies and all eyes on you.

▶ 2. Let your students know you will give directions first and will then ask them to move quietly. Be sure they understand that you expect no one to move until you give directions, and those unable to adhere will cause everyone to begin again. Be sure to stop if anyone jumps the gun on your directions. Failing to do so will eventually limit the effectiveness of your efforts at quiet, orderly transitions.

▶ 3. If several groups of students need to move, allow only one group at a time to go, and wait until those students are settled according to your expectations. Compliment students, if they warrant it. Then move the remaining students, one group at a time. Quiet and orderly transitioning can help set the tone for your lesson, and make it more likely your students will settle and begin in a timely manner. Don't forget the students left at their desks to work, if any. They should be supplied with seatwork that can be done independently and should have clear instructions about sharpening pencils, using the bathroom, and anything else that could be disruptive to your group lesson.

▶ 4. Be sure to repeat instructions, and clarify if necessary. Praise students who are transitioning appropriately. Point out appropriate actions as you give a compliment: "I like the way Javon has picked up his chair and is quietly carrying it to the math table."

▶ 5. When group lessons are completed, use the same strategy to send students back to their desks. This strategy may take time and seem laborious at first, but as students become clear about your expectations, things will move more quickly. Less time will be wasted transitioning, and students will be settled and ready to begin work.

Moving for Group Learning Activities

Do you wish you were a magician when moving your students into small groups for a lesson? There is no magic wand available for you, but here's an idea that just might do the trick.

▶ 1. Be sure you have planned your moving strategy ahead of time so you know exactly how it will go. When giving directions, be sure you have the attention of all students. Using one of the techniques from the previous strategy can work well. Tell them you will explain how you want them to move, and then ask them to move one group, table, section, or row at a time. Do not allow the entire class to move all at once as this can only result in chaos.

▶ 2. Using a number system for the students in your classroom can be one good method of making up groups of any size. Drawing arbitrary numbers from a hat or forming small groups using numerical order are just two ways numbers can be useful. Be sure to tell your students what method you will use, and vary it from time to time. You may even want to do a sociogram at sometime during the year to give children an opportunity to work with friends.

▶ 3. When you are ready to break up, move only a small number of students at a time. Stress moving quietly by picking up chairs or desks—you do not want to hear furniture scraping and screeching on the floor. As the first students move, praise those complying with your directions. When they are settled, reiterate the directions for the second group. Move groups separately, waiting until each is settled and quiet before going on to the next one.

▶ 4. Moving students in a quiet and orderly manner helps set the stage for an easier to manage, more successful, small group or cooperative learning session. The chaos that results from allowing the entire class to move all at once often spills over to the lesson, and you may find you spend a great deal of learning time trying to stop the inappropriate behavior that began during transition time.

One Classroom to Another

Going to art, gym, music, and other special classes are transitioning times, too. Do you shudder when the clock tells you it's time to go? Think "quiet and orderly," and the trips will be much less painful.

▶ 1. It's a good idea to post a listing of special classes and when they occur throughout the week. This helps you and your students to get mentally, as well as physically, prepared on time.

▶ 2. It's also important to gauge the time it takes to wrap up whatever lesson you are having and prepare to move students to a special class. At first, be sure to allot more than enough time, because things move more slowly when changes are new at the beginning of the year. Does the time of day indicate that a stop at the bathroom might be in order before or after the special class? If so, be sure to include that in your planned transitioning time.

▶ 3. As in other transitioning situations, begin by giving students a reminder that in just a few minutes, they will be going to gym, art, or another special class. Indicate that it is time to begin putting things away and that you will know students are ready when desks are clear and eyes are on you. Remind students about lining up quietly in line order and say you will not move until everyone is settled and ready.

▶ 4. While you are waiting to go, it's a good time to review your expectations for your students in their special class. They need to know you are working with the specialist teacher to ensure appropriate behavior in the classroom and that you will not hesitate to provide consequences for anyone who misbehaves. While moving through hallways, your students should follow the procedures described in Chapter 6, Entering School and Line Order. If you do not remain with your students during the special class, it may be useful, especially at the start of the year, to remain long enough to help the specialist settle the class. Reminders from you about rewards or other appropriate consequences may be helpful also.

▶ 5. Because some special classes are more loosely structured than a regular classroom—gym, for example—you will want to be sure students are quiet and orderly before you enter the hallway and begin the return trip to your room. You may need to remind them about expectations for their hands, feet, and mouths. You may need to stop more frequently in the hallway on the return trip to help students calm down and regain control. This will go a long way in ensuring a peaceful entrance to your classroom and a quicker, quieter start to your next activity.

If you have special education students in your classroom, you should be aware that transitions of any kind can often be difficult for them. Using a consistent format for your transitions is important and can alleviate disruptive behavior. Consider putting your daily schedule on the board regularly so your students know what will happen when. This may be of significant benefit to your special education students. Seating those students among others who can maintain good control and focus during transition times may be helpful. You may need to find a spot in line for some special education students between classmates with good self-control. This may encourage and enable better behavior.

Taking Care of Classroom Business

This chapter covers some of the meat and potatoes of developing your classroom management system. Creating strategies for the topics in this chapter is a real must for teachers who have high expectations for learning during the school year. Remember, these ideas can be changed and modified to fit your particular classroom needs—the most important thing is that you have workable strategies in place.

Chapter Outline

- Entering School
- Entering the Classroom
- Beginning the Day
- Absenteeism
- Homework Collection
- Failure to Do Homework
- Line Order
- Bathroom Procedure

- Drinks
- Classroom Rules
- Indoor Recess
- Reentering the Classroom After Lunch and Recess
- Ending the Day
- Pencil Sharpening
- Gum, Candy, and Other Forbidden Edibles

Entering School

Does bringing your class into the building put a monkey wrench in your day before it even begins? Here's an idea that will set the scene for success.

▶ 1. If your school rules don't include a spot for students to gather and line up before entering, designate one yourself.

▶ 2. Be at that spot *before* the bell rings for students to come in, reminding students to be in their special place in line preparing to come in with quiet mouths and hands to themselves. *Do not* enter the building with your students until they are conforming to your set rules for entering school and walking in the halls. Decide on a method of dealing with those who do not comply; for example, bring them to the front of the line or have them walk with you. Begin by walking backwards, facing the line, and then position yourself so you can see the entire line.

▶ 3. It's a good idea to have a clipboard with a classroom list so you can give positive points to those who conform, verbally praising those students. This is also a good way to remember the names of students who lose privileges. Remind those students of loss of rewards, free time, and so forth.

▶ 4. As you walk into school and through the halls, be sure to position yourself so that you can see the entire line, complimenting students who comply and reminding those who don't. Use anchors for the line, such as walking under the hall lights or on a certain line on the floor. Have designated spots where the line stops, as it is easier to control when you can stop them and regroup if necessary. When you reach your classroom, stop the line, and remind students of your expectations as they hang up their coats and school bags and enter the classroom. Position yourself someplace where you can see both the classroom and the hallway or coat area and monitor activities in both places.

▶ 5. If your school's policy is for students to enter the building on their own, you will want to set some expectations for lining up outside your classroom and entering it. If you have a line order, expect the students to line up accordingly. Do not enter the classroom until they are quiet and settled. Before they enter, remind students of how they are to go in and what they will be expected to do once at their desks. Direct them to hang up coats, book bags, and so on in a quiet, orderly manner. Position yourself someplace where you can see both the room and the hallway or coat area and monitor activities in both places.

Entering the Classroom

Do your students enter the classroom like a herd of elephants? Here is a strategy to ensure that chaos is a thing of the past as your students begin the day.

▶ 1. As your students are hanging up their coats, position yourself so that you can see both the hallway or coat room and the classroom while you remind students what your expectations are for them in both places.

▶ 2. Be sure to greet students with "Good morning," or another pleasant phrase, as they enter the room. Expect a response from them (a teachable moment for this important social skill that many of our students don't practice).

▶ 3. Remind those in the hall that you expect them to hang up their coats, gather their things quickly and quietly, and enter the room. Keep your ears open for inappropriate behavior of hallway stragglers, and interrupt your routine, if necessary, to deal with them.

▶ 4. Remind those already in the classroom of your expectations as they begin the day.

▶ 5. Praise the class for entering and following opening-of-the-day procedures. If you have implemented a whole-class reward system, a quiet beginning of the day may be a time you want to reward with a classroom point. (Refer to Chapter 8, Rewards.)

Beginning the Day

Do you have a difficult time settling students in your classroom as they begin the morning? Here's an idea that may be just the answer for this hair-pulling time for you.

▶ 1. Before students go to their desks or gather quietly on the carpet, you must have set expectations for lunch count, attendance, turning in homework, and so forth, which the students know and understand. Here are two quick and effective lunch count and attendance ideas:

    a. On a large poster or bulletin board, arrange students' names in line order. Be sure the names are movable in case of changes. You may want to laminate your line order chart and the names. Then use small Velcro tabs or sticky gum to attach the names to the chart. Have students clip in with colored clothespins that correspond with the lunch count (e.g., blue for hot lunch, pink for cold, etc.). At a glance, missing clothespins will indicate absentees.

    b. Hang a *clear* pocket shoe holder on a bulletin board or near a gathering spot (Figure 6.1). Label the top three pockets with identifying pictures of home, hot lunch, or cold lunch. The six remaining pockets below are color coded with six different colors. Divide the class by color codes (five to six children, maximum, per color, so students

Figure 6.1 Pocket Shoe Bag for Tracking Which Students
Eat Lunch at Home and Which Have a Hot or Cold Lunch at School

can more easily find their own names), and make a card stock strip with each child's name and color on it. Place strips in corresponding color pockets. Each child places her or his color-coded name card in the appropriate lunch pocket. At a glance, the name cards left in color-coded pockets indicate absentees.

▶ 2. Most students are not self-directed enough to come into the classroom in the morning and find something constructive to do until the teacher begins the first activity. You need to provide it for them.

▶ 3. No matter what you choose for your students, from gathering quietly on a carpet to doing assigned work, be sure they understand your expectations, and be sure you are consistent in enforcing them.

▶ 4. If you assign journals, board work, a worksheet, or some other task, have it on their desks or at an easy pick-up point *before* they enter the room. This should be work that takes very little explanation from you—something they can settle down to do quickly and quietly with a pencil as the only necessary tool.

▶ 5. It is also very important that students are held responsible for this work. It should be shared or corrected by you or in class daily so students take the assignment seriously. Then students will be encouraged to settle quickly each morning to complete their work, knowing they will be held responsible for it in some way. Be sure to provide directions for students when they have completed their work, such as where to place it, what to do until others have finished, and so forth.

Numerous alternatives when deciding what to choose for initial morning work include journals, seatwork, board work, or a lesson on the overhead projector. (Using your overhead projector allows you to save for reuse any materials you prepare.) The following suggestions are just a few ideas that can be effective in settling students when they enter your classroom in the morning.

▶ 1. Open-ended stem for silent journal writing, such as

    a. Yesterday when I got home from school . . .

    b. If I were an astronaut, this is what I'd see in space . . .

    c. The character I like best in the story we are reading now is . . .

    d. These are things I like to do outside when it snows . . .

▶ 2. Daily oral language (DOL) or sentence stumpers, which challenge students to correct grade-level grammar and punctuation errors in sentences.

▶ 3. Math mysteries, which review previously taught math skills. These can stand alone or can be combined with DOL.

▶ 4. Worksheets to review the following:

    a. Spelling

    b. Penmanship

    c. Word scrambles or puzzles

    d. A reading comprehension passage, with some multiple-choice or short-answer questions

    e. Seasonally related activities

If you have special education students in your classroom at the beginning of the school day, be sure you have appropriate assigned work for them to do. Consult with the special education teacher to be sure that the board work, worksheet, or other task is something that can successfully be completed independently by these students.

Absenteeism

Do too many empty seats in your classroom make you feel like an actor with a dwindling audience? Chronically absent students are of significant concern to any teacher. There are some things you can do yourself as well as with the assistance of school support staff to address this serious problem. Read on.

► 1. One of the first things to remember is that in many instances, your absent students may have little or no control over whether or not they get to school on any given day. This is especially true for younger children, who may include those from kindergarten to third grade. This is only one important reason that communication with parents on a consistent basis is extremely important. Your efforts to establish a cordial, working relationship with parents can provide an avenue for you to express your concern about the absent student.

► 2. Unfortunately, the reality often is that, for whatever reason, it is often difficult to make contact with some parents. If there is no home phone, perhaps there is a work number where you can leave a message or speak briefly to the parent. It may be possible that a neighbor or other family member's phone number can be provided for you. If contact by phone is not possible, notes home—either mailed or sent home via the student or a responsible sibling—may work. You should be sure to document any efforts you have made to reach parents as well as whether or not they have responded.

► 3. Most school districts have policies on chronic absenteeism and a sequence for implementing them. Often, office staff will be the first ones to make parent contact after a student has been chronically absent. At times, however, these students can fall through the cracks. For this reason, it is very important for you as the teacher to keep track of students who are frequently not at school. Contact the office for information and help when a student has had many absences over a 2- or 3-week period. (The length of time before absence becomes a concern may differ among school districts, so check the policy in yours.)

► 4. If you feel you need further assistance beyond what the office staff can offer, you may want to contact your school social worker. If you have been unable to reach the parents, the social worker may be able to make a home visit, and it may be possible for you to accompany the social worker if you so desire. Check with your principal. A visit by the social worker can often be very revealing and offer some good insight as to how and why the home situation may be affecting the student's attendance.

► 5. Within your classroom, encouraging good attendance is, of course, important. Often schoolwide attendance recognition is given to rooms that have had the greatest number of students present over a week, a month, or more, and special, fun activities are planned as a reward. These are good ideas, but, again, keep in mind that in many cases, the students themselves may not be responsible for their absences.

Homework Collection

Is collecting homework a hellish task for you? Is your desk inundated with paper each morning as your students turn in their assignments? Here's how to turn chaos into order.

▶ 1. No matter if you decide to send homework home daily, weekly, or in the form of a monthly project, you must set clear expectations for these assignments. Be sure students have an absolutely clear understanding of directions before you send the work home. Be realistic, and keep in mind that many students get little or no assistance with homework, so be sure assignments require a minimum of materials and can be completed independently.

▶ 2. Designate an area for homework collection, and label the baskets with homework subjects. Remind students to turn their work in as soon as they enter the classroom in the morning.

▶ 3. Give students concrete consequences for late or undone assignments. They can spend recess time catching up or miss free time or other rewards when homework is consistently missing. After a week, that assignment receives a zero unless the student has a legitimate excuse.

▶ 4. Devise a specific method for keeping track of students' assignments. For example, if students are given permanent numbers, assign someone to each subject basket, and have that person order the homework using the numbers matching the permanent number assignments. No paper should be accepted without a name and number in the heading.

▶ 5. Once the papers are ordered by number, it takes only a few minutes to jot down the names of students whose papers are missing. Referring to your line order or permanent number list, you can quickly record the numbers of those missing assignments.

Here are some suggestions that can help make homework—going home or coming back to school—a more painless task for both you and your students. Several of these ideas may be particularly applicable to kindergarten or early primary-age children.

▶ 1. Use zipper lock bags for books that go home, to extend the life of the book and to hold materials and worksheets connected to the story.

▶ 2. Use a pocket folder or zipper lock bag to hold homework, flyers, and newsletters.

▶ 3. In kindergarten or early primary classes, a number of items often are routinely taken home and returned. A form letter listing these items can be created so that just the child's name can be added, with items circled that need to be returned.

▶ 4. Create a check-off class list for items that are so important you will want to verify that they have been returned.

▶ 5. Dishpans and baskets can be labeled with a picture or color coded to identify the objects to be placed inside. (Large dishpans work best because they can hold more items than most baskets.) As children enter the classroom, they can independently sort and return such items as library books, homework books, daily homework pocket folders, and permission slips or other important papers. If young children have difficulty sorting items returned at the beginning of the year, use just two boxes or baskets—one for homework and one for all other returns. An easy check of homework with one to three items is to have the children hold up the work; you will easily see which students have and have not done the work.

If you have special education students in you classroom, you may want to consult with the special education teacher and decide whether only one or both of you will assign homework. One of your aims regarding homework for all your students should be that they can successfully complete it by themselves in a reasonable amount of time. These are important things you will want to discuss with the special education teacher.

Failure to Do Homework

"The dog ate my homework." Is this only one among many excuses you hear on a regular basis from a certain group of students who never seem to be able to return their homework? Here are some strategies you can implement to encourage your students to keep those assignments away from the dog.

▶ 1. There are some important things to remember regarding homework you assign. Be sure your students have the materials at home to complete the assignments. If they don't have the things they need—such as pencils, crayons, and scissors—they can't finish their work. Be sure you assign work that the students can complete independently. There may be some children who have no one at home to help them because of a language barrier or illiteracy. Your students should not be penalized if they cannot do the assignment on their own. Assign reasonable amounts of homework. Remember, you want students to be able to be successful in completing and returning their work. If you have special education students in your classroom, be sure to consult with the special education teacher about how homework will be assigned to these students.

▶ 2. Devise a way to be sure that the homework actually does go home. Provide mailboxes (see Chapter 7 under the heading Mailboxes on page 68) or some other way of making sure student work is in one place in preparation to be taken home. You may want to organize a way that homework gets from the mailbox to the students' backpacks to ensure the greatest chance for it to arrive home. It may be possible for you to have students bring backpacks into the classroom and then place work from their mailboxes directly into them.

▶ 3. You may want to create some reward programs to encourage your students to bring in their completed work. Some teachers create homework charts that are posted and visible in the classroom. Small rewards are given to those who return the work over designated periods of time. Homework Lotto allows each student to place a ticket with her or his name on it in a bowl each time that student's homework is on time. Several names are drawn at the end of the week, and these students receive a variety of small rewards. There are many ways you can encourage your students to be responsible about their work. You may even want to ask them as a group what kind of reward program you could devise that would encourage them to turn in homework.

▶ 4. Don't forget the value of keeping the parents informed about what is happening in your classroom on a regular basis. A classroom newsletter is one way to do this (see Chapter 2 under the heading Connecting with Parents—Classroom Newsletters on page 13). The newsletter can also serve as a vehicle to list the names of those students who have completed their homework all week. Students will be proud to show off their names to their parents, and it won't matter if the parents can read or not—their child will be delighted to read it to them.

▶ 5. Some teachers find weekly homework packets to be more successful than daily assignments. Students receive the work at the beginning of each week and have until week's end to complete it and turn it in. During the week, many teachers offer assistance to students who may be having difficulty with the work. Some even give students time during the school day to work on it. This can offer an opportunity for those students who might, for whatever reason, be unable to finish their homework at home.

Line Order

Does chaos reign when your class lines up to travel in the hallway? Here's one teacher-tested method that can really help.

▶ 1. When preparing students to line up, call small groups of students (five to seven) to line up by assigned numbers, by table numbers, by colors, by alphabetical order, or by random teacher selection. If you choose a set order of any kind, be sure you have a list, and post the list that all your students can see to avoid confusion and arguing.

▶ 2. If you see any combination of students who seem to be a potential problem, separate them.

▶ 3. If the first group of students called does not line up appropriately, have them return to their seats and try again. Try calling another group to see if they can model the correct behavior.

▶ 4. Praise groups of students for knowing line basics: arms at sides or folded in front, lips together, face forward.

Figure 6.2 List Showing Students' Order in Line

Line Order

1. Sam Harmon
2. Jenny Smith
3. Maxwell Rios
4. Violet Marcks
5. Anthony Lesher
6. Rachel Evans
7. Harry Swick
8. Haley Sporek
9. Jack Olstinski

▶ 5. When the entire group is ready, you can begin to move. Remind line leaders of anchors and designated stopping points.

Have students practice lining up frequently during the first month of school. Challenge them to line up silently and quickly, reinforcing line basics.

If you choose to use a number order for lining up, you will find it to be an organizer and time-saver extraordinaire.

Assigning numbers is a real time-saver for

a. Collecting homework labeled with a name and number

b. Assigning lockers

c. Breaking into groups for field trips or assigning to group leaders

d. Collecting money for any purpose

e. Taking lunch count

f. Selecting person of the week by drawing numbers

g. Determining a computer or other special activity schedule when availability is limited

h. Choosing students arbitrarily for any group or individual activity

Bathroom Procedure

Do you dread those trips with students to the bathroom? Does it take far too long and usually involve horseplay or worse? Try this teacher-tested idea, and see if things improve.

▶ 1. First, be sure to review your expectations for line basics, hall behavior, and bathroom behavior. Bathroom rules should include using the bathroom quickly and quietly and washing hands thoroughly. Discuss them with your class as many times as necessary (as well as reviewing them throughout the year). You may also want to take a clipboard to keep track of students who are following your directions so you can give individual rewards or other consequences—especially at the beginning of the year.

▶ 2. Be sure you have already decided how you will implement this procedure. For example:

a. Limit class bathroom breaks during the day. Combine them with hallway traveling: for example, on the way to or from lunch or specialists. The only individual exceptions should be legitimate emergencies.

b. If you have a helper in your classroom sometime during the day, you may want to take your class during this time. You may want to send students who are finished back to class with your assistant if you feel that person is capable of handling this task. This avoids the possibility of losing control of a long line of students who are waiting. If you have no one to help, you may be able to take your class at the same time as another group so that you and the other teacher can divide up the boys and girls, each accompanying one group.

c. If you have younger children, you may be able to enlist the help of a trustworthy, upper-grade student to monitor one group while you handle the other.

▶ 3. Bathroom expectations should include lips together, hand washing, and getting out quickly and quietly. You will want to send a limited number, no more than two or three, into the bathroom at the same time, and remember to avoid troublesome combinations.

▶ 4. Expect orderly lines while waiting and when finished. Waiting in line can also be teaching time.

▶ 5. Remember to praise students who have done a good job. This would be an excellent reward time for appropriate class behavior. (See Chapter 8, Rewards.)

Waiting time is teaching time, whether outside the bathrooms, in hallways, on field trips (waiting for busses and so forth), or waiting for specialists. This is an opportunity to avoid behavior problems as you reinforce appropriate behavior. Possible strategies:

1. Counting by 2s, 5s, 10s, and so on
2. Reading poems or singing songs—new and old favorites
3. Clapping rhythmic patterns by listening and repeating
4. Practicing science, social studies, math facts, or letter sounds
5. Exercising arm, shoulder, hand, and head

These are also great strategies to get stragglers to their seats or carpet and for redirecting a noisy group so that you can begin your lesson.

Drinks

Does the pushing, shoving, and horseplay involved with students' getting a drink at the water fountain make you cringe? A game plan can really eliminate problems and calm those troubled waters.

▶ 1. Whether you are offering drinks of water after recess, during a bathroom break, or at another time when you are in the hall with your students, have a plan, and be sure they know your expectations.

▶ 2. You can choose to use your line order, and allow only two children at the water fountain at a time. The remainder of the class should remain in line quietly.

▶ 3. You will want to limit the time a student can continue to drink at the water fountain. You can do this by simply telling students you will count to five (or whatever number you feel is adequate), at which time, you will expect them to be finished. Those who continue drinking will miss the opportunity the next time. (Initially, you may need a pad and pencil for name taking, to indicate that you intend to make your rule stick.)

▶ 4. Those students in line who cannot remain quiet forfeit their chance to have a drink. If you enforce this plan immediately and stick to it, you greatly increase your chances of having problem-free drink time for the year.

▶ 5. Remember to praise students who have done a good job. This would be an excellent reward time for appropriate class behavior. (See Chapter 8, Rewards.)

Classroom Rules

It's not the army—but there must be rules. Be sure they are measurable and reasonable. With your direction, involve the kids in creating them. Here are some tried and true suggestions.

▶ 1. It is imperative that you spend time during the first days and weeks of school talking about your expectations for appropriate classroom behavior. Allow students to help you brainstorm a list of *positively* stated classroom rules early in the first week.

▶ 2. After students have had ample time to brainstorm, begin to organize their suggestions beneath this core of (no more than) *five* necessary rules:

    a. Raise your hand, and wait patiently to be called on; listen while others talk.

    b. Use proper language (G-rated, as in the movies).

    c. Remain seated unless you have permission to move.

    d. Keep your hands and feet to yourself.

    e. Listen, and carefully follow directions.

    You will find most of the students' ideas will fit under these five rules.

▶ 3. Post your classroom rules where they can be easily read, referred to, and reviewed often, especially during the first few weeks of school. Be sure to send home a list of your rules so family members are aware of them also.

▶ 4. Praise students who abide by your classroom rules, and have fair, consistent expectations for *all* students.

▶ 5. Prepare and post clear consequences for students who choose not to comply. (See Chapter 9, Consequences.)

Indoor Recess

The weather outside is frightful, but indoor recess isn't so delightful. Structure here—like most other places in school—is the key.

▶ 1. At the beginning of the school year, develop a plan as to how you will handle your class or whatever group of students land in your room during indoor recess. (If your school already has a procedure, then you're all set.)

▶ 2. First of all, realize that indoor recess doesn't entitle students to a free-for-all. It needs to be organized and structured just as any in-school activity. Limit choices to three or four. For example: quiet table games, reading, drawing, and computers. If possible, let your students make their selection earlier in the day, and post it on the board or in another visible place. If prior choice isn't possible, have students enter the room and sit down quietly. Then you can quickly list choices, and students can select. For younger children, you may choose to use a clothespin chart—as students enter the room, they can clip their clothespins next to the words or a picture of the activity. The teacher can also do this ahead of time as the children decide what they want to do. Then, when they enter, they need only to look for their name as a reminder. (Be cautious about activities such as writing on the chalkboard, using art supplies, or active games. Without strict adult supervision, these activities can get out of hand.)

▶ 3. Make sure rules are clear. They should include whispering or very quiet talking, staying in assigned area, and raising hands for questions or help. Changing activities should happen only with your permission and supervision.

▶ 4. You need to patrol the room and supervise just as in any activity. Be sure to keep the noise level down, as an increase in volume often indicates that things are beginning to get out of control.

▶ 5. About a minute or so before clean-up time, tell students to finish whatever they are doing because they will have about 5 minutes before the bell rings to clean up. Circulate around the room when students are cleaning up, urging them to do so quickly and quietly. Compliment students who comply. Be sure you have alternative activities for students who cannot follow indoor recess directions. These could include writing assignments or anything other than joining in the recess fun.

Reentering the Classroom After Lunch and Recess

Does the herd-of-elephant syndrome occur once again when your students stampede into the classroom after lunchtime or recess? Your expectations and some simple preparations can make a real difference.

▶ 1. Be sure to use your strategy for entering school with your students (see Entering School on page 49) again when reentering the building after lunchtime or recess. This will be very helpful in beginning to settle them so you can start your academic activities.

▶ 2. Compliment students who walk in quietly and begin the assigned task right away. Be sure to choose something students can do with no additional instructions so that they can begin immediately. Writing in journals, reading library books, and completing seatwork are some suggestions.

▶ 3. It's a good idea to have whatever assignment you've chosen ready to go on each student's desk *before* they enter the room. This means that before your students leave, journals or library books must be on their desks or seatwork should be distributed. This greatly minimizes the opportunity for disruption once students reenter, because they don't need to rummage through desks or wander around the room.

▶ 4. Circulate around the room, compliment students who continue to work quietly, and make sure all students are engaged in the activity. This may be a time you can play a tape of quiet, enjoyable music for a calming effect. You may also want to use this time for afternoon pencil sharpening. Do not begin the next activity until you feel your students have recovered from the lunch, recess, or other break. Then follow the idea in Chapter 5 for a smooth transition into the next activity.

Ending the Day

You want to end the day in a quiet, orderly fashion—your students have other ideas. Here's a suggestion that can help ensure your peace of mind.

▶ 1. During your quiet end-of-the day activity, you can dismiss students one group at a time to quietly get their coats and schoolbags, check their mailboxes, and return to their desks or assigned spots. They can pack their homework and then return to the quiet activity. You may need to position yourself at the door to supervise the hallway or coatroom and the class-room. The emphasis during this time remains quiet order. Or students could already have coats and book bags hung on chairs before you begin the organized end-of-day activity.

▶ 2. You need to establish an end-of-day routine that is quiet and orderly. Daily journal writing, silent reading, computer time, teacher reading aloud—any calming activity—is the sane choice for day's end.

▶ 3. Model your expectations by quietly reading, writing in your journal, or doing other work at your desk or in another place visible to all your students. Later in the year, when a stable end-of-day routine is in place, you are free to tutor or read with small groups or individuals, write notes to parents, pass out school information, or do whatever else needs to be done.

▶ 4. Leave enough time for the following activities—usually between 5 and 15 minutes, depending on the age of your students. All corrected work and school notes should be packed into a take-home folder for parents to check every night. Make last minute reminders about field trips, special projects, or assignments due. When the bell rings, call quiet and ready students to line up, and implement your hallway rules as you walk to the bus or outside.

▶ 5. If you have both bus riders and walkers at your school, and there is no format already in place, have a system for taking both to their designated areas. Perhaps you can buddy with another teacher—one taking the students who walk and the other escorting bussed students to their lines.

The day for kindergarten or early primary children should also end quietly. Here are some suggestions. Determine whether you would like children in an independent, quiet activity in order to write notes, clean up, and so forth, or if you will be involved with them. Independent activities could include the following (be sure to model them first):

▶ 1. A capable student holds a storybook and turns the pages as the tape tells the story.

▶ 2. Children gather on the carpet and read softly, choosing books from tubs near the carpet.

▶ 3. Upper-grade book buddies can read independently with the children.

Teacher-directed activities could include the following:

▶ 1. Introduce a new unit or following day's activity using a story, puppet, or objects to pass around, to excite the children about coming to school tomorrow. Couple this with a letter asking that children bring certain things to school or observe something at home relevant to the activity.

▶ 2. Read a story, sing a favorite song, or recite poetry.

▶ 3. Select some children to read their journals to the class.

If your weekly schedule includes a special class immediately before lunch, recess, or dismissal, here are some suggestions that can smooth that difficult transition time. The following are some orderly routines for before lunch and recess, which can help:

▶ 1. Carry all lunches in a large box or laundry basket (labeled in indelible ink with your name and room number) to the special class.

▶ 2. Have children bring outer clothing, boots, and so forth to the special class.

▶ 3. Have children use the bathroom on the way to the special class.

▶ 4. Give lunch tickets to the special teacher to pass out as the children leave (or, if you meet the students at the end of class, pass them out yourself).

Routines that can expedite the end of your day include these:

▶ 1. Have students clean their desks and the room before you leave.

▶ 2. Be sure all homework, notes, and so forth are in students' backpacks before you leave for the special class.

▶ 3. Have students put on boots, snow pants, and so on before going to a special class (other than gym) and bring outer clothing, backpacks, and whatever else is needed to the special class.

Pencil Sharpening

Are you plagued with a constant barrage of students sharpening pencils while you are delivering yet another scintillating lesson? Consistently follow this rule in the a.m. and p.m. for grind-free teaching.

▶ 1. Require that all students have at least two pencils. Most schools sell supplies, or you can sell pencils at your classroom store. See Chapter 7, Supplies.

▶ 2. Let students know that pencil sharpening is allowed during a limited time period—15 minutes to a half hour—in the morning and in the afternoon.

▶ 3. Let students know that only *one* person is allowed at the sharpener at a time. You may need to ask who needs to sharpen pencils and allow turns by calling names if students are unable to do this in an orderly manner by themselves.

▶ 4. Instruct students to *wait* until the sharpener is free before *walking* to use it.

▶ 5. Be firm and consistent with the enforcement of this rule. Students will learn when pencil sharpening is appropriate and to respect you when you are teaching.

Gum, Candy, and Other Forbidden Edibles

Are your students constantly on a sugar high from all the candy they're treating themselves with during class? Here's what four out of five dentists and teachers recommend to squelch an unwanted candy epidemic in your classroom.

▶ 1. Be sure to find out what your school policy is regarding edible treats so you will know when and if they are ever acceptable. Make it clear to students that treating themselves to candy and gum in your classroom is not acceptable unless you have given permission. If students bring a treat, there must be enough for *everyone* in class.

▶ 2. When you catch students with candy or gum, have them throw it away, watching to be sure it has actually been discarded; then remind them of your no-candy, no-gum policy. (This should include the teacher—you are the role model.)

▶ 3. If a student is caught again, write the name down on a skip-treat list.

▶ 4. Although it will be difficult, the next time you treat the class, skip any repeat offenders and remind them that they have already had their treats—the ones with which they were previously caught. You should not have to do this too many times before everyone gets the idea.

▶ 5. This will nearly always guarantee that once students have been skipped, their names rarely turn up on the skip-treat list again.

HEY TEACHER—
IS SPIKE NON-SCHOOL-
RELATED MATERIAL?

7

Organizational Time

Housekeeping within your classroom may seem insignificant compared to the many other concerns you have. But don't underestimate the importance of planning and implementing some ideas in this chapter, aimed at keeping you and your room in good order. An organized classroom makes it easier for you to function and also helps hold your students responsible for their own assignments, materials, and supplies—an important lesson that can be taught through these organizational time (OT) strategies.

Chapter Outline

■ Desk Cleaning

■ Supplies

■ Mailboxes

■ Non-School-Related Materials

Desk Cleaning

Do the words *tornado alley* come to mind when you think about the inside of the desks of many of your students? You need to take control of the mess so that your students can take better control of their assignments. Here's how.

▶ 1. At the beginning of the year, decide on a time during the day when you will have an OT—that is, a time to clean out and rearrange desk contents. Sometime near the end of the day may work best. At first, you will need to do this frequently—until your students understand your expectations for their desks. Later in the year, you may need to do this only once a week or so.

▶ 2. Set your expectations. Post a chart for OT including these directions:

    a. Take everything out of your desk.

    b. Recycle or throw away anything you do not want or need for school. Ask the teacher if you are not sure about what to do with something.

    c. Put non-school-related materials on your desk to take home today.

    d. Organize your school materials neatly in your desk.

    e. Raise your hand to let your teacher know you are ready for desk inspection.

▶ 3. Do not fail to inspect every desk. Not doing so will send the message that you don't follow through on expectations.

▶ 4. In a further attempt to help students, especially older ones, organize their desk contents, you may want them to have different-color pocket folders for different subjects, projects, or assignments. Regular reminders during the day to put assigned work in its proper folder will help students keep better track of things they need and things that can be taken home or recycled.

Supplies

Is the almighty yet elusive pencil the bane of your existence? Are you constantly looking for ways to keep your students supplied with the materials they need for their work, but without much success? Here are some helpful hints to consider.

▶ 1. There are always students who seem to have a limited sense of responsibility regarding materials they need for school. Pencils are usually the biggest problem. You need to make your policy regarding supplies clear during the first week of school. This policy should not include lending students your own supplies.

▶ 2. One solution to the supplies problem is to have your own supply store. Often, near the end of summer, discount and other stores will have school supplies on sale for very low prices. This is a good time for you to stock up on pencils, erasers, folders, loose-leaf paper, and notebooks. You can post a list of supplies and prices in your classroom, and have your store open at certain times. Students from third grade on up can run the store for you, and it becomes a hands-on math lesson. Tell your students they can purchase supplies or borrow from other students if they do not have needed materials—these are their two choices. Children could also earn points towards buying the necessary supplies by doing jobs for the teacher.

▶ 3. Another option that can work well, especially in lower elementary grades, is to place a basket on each desk group containing crayons and enough pencils for everyone in the group. Students understand that these materials must be returned to the baskets when not in use. You can spot-check each basket periodically during the day to be sure the proper number of pencils and crayons remain inside; or designate someone in the group to count and report to you.

▶ 4. Crayons can also be a problem. You may want to keep them yourself and allow students to have them only when doing projects where they are needed. Or younger children can keep crayons in zipper lock bags in their cubbies or in baskets on tables or in areas where needed. Counting crayons before and after a project is also a good math exercise for younger students. Another good idea is to have a container of used crayons as replacements when needed. They can be collected from students themselves as they discard old, broken crayons throughout the year. Also, at year's end, students will often throw them away—collect them yourself for next year.

▶ 5. Certain items—such as red pencils, watercolor paints, glue, or scissors—may be needed only occasionally. It is usually best to order enough of these materials for everyone in your class and then distribute them only when they are needed for specific projects. Collect the materials when the project is finished, making sure to collect the same number of items you distributed.

If you have special education students in your classroom, you should be aware that some of them may have a difficult time keeping their desks and other materials organized. Again, it is important for you to have a copy of the child's individual education plan (IEP) to see if this is a concern. Consulting with the special education teacher may reveal ways to help the student stay organized. Many teachers have successful ways to help students keep supplies and information where they can be easily accessed. Notebooks and color-coded pocket folders for each subject will enable some special education students to keep important work at hand. You may want to keep extra pencils, crayons, or other supplies belonging to the student at your desk so they aren't misplaced or lost. Finding a method that works—for those students that need help staying organized—can go a long way in ensuring academic success.

Mailboxes

How can you be sure every student receives copies of the seemingly endless paper flow generated by your school office—or that absent students have all the work they missed? Here's a sure-fire solution.

▶ 1. Student mailboxes are a wonderful way to solve your paper crunch problem. Most supply catalogues available in your school office will carry some type of cardboard storage box item.

▶ 2. You can order enough for each student in your classroom, and stack them in an easily accessible spot. Label each box and put them in alphabetical order or any order that makes sense to you and your students.

▶ 3. You may decide to have a student mailperson to handle daily deliveries of notes and homework. Then choose a specific time of the day—usually

Figure 7.1 How to Make Student Mailboxes from Shoeboxes

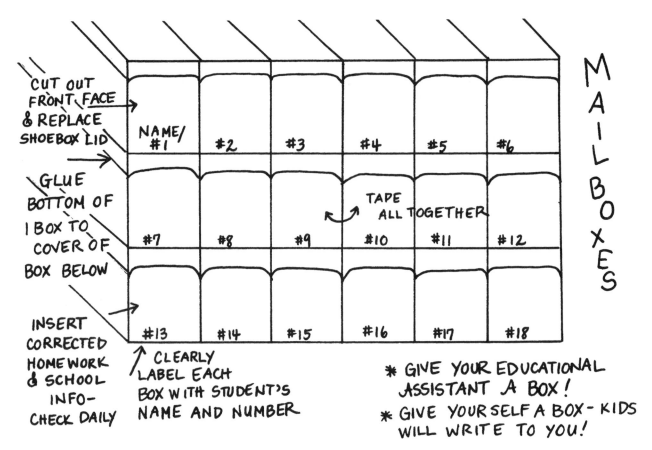

CUT OUT FRONT FACE & REPLACE SHOEBOX LID

GLUE BOTTOM OF 1 BOX TO COVER OF BOX BELOW

INSERT CORRECTED HOMEWORK & SCHOOL INFO— CHECK DAILY

NAME/ #1   #2   #3   #4   #5   #6

#7   #8   #9   #10   #11   #12

TAPE ALL TOGETHER

#13   #14   #15   #16   #17   #18

↑ CLEARLY LABEL EACH BOX WITH STUDENT'S NAME AND NUMBER

MAILBOXES

* GIVE YOUR EDUCATIONAL ASSISTANT A BOX!
* GIVE YOURSELF A BOX - KIDS WILL WRITE TO YOU!

day's end works best—to have students retrieve their mail or to have the mailperson distribute it.

▶ 4. If you don't have access to storage boxes of this type, have each student bring a shoebox. One short end can be cut out, and then the shoeboxes can be stacked and taped together and used in the same way (Figure 7.1). Plastic crates that hold hanging file folders can also serve as mailboxes with students' names slipped in the plastic tabs on the folders. This one-time investment can be used year after year. Shoe bags can also serve as permanent mailboxes to be used from year to year.

▶ 5. If mailboxes are not feasible for your students, handouts can be placed directly into open schoolbags at the end of the day. If some students don't have school bags, purchase some heavy-duty, gallon-sized, zipper lock, freezer bags labeled with the child's name. These can serve just as well and will protect papers and books from the elements.

Non-School-Related Materials

Do your students think playtime extends to the classroom? If you are always confiscating non-school-related materials, here's suggestion that should reduce this problem to a trickle.

▶ 1. At the beginning of the year (although it's never too late to start this) discuss your policy on toys and other forbidden materials in your classroom. Also discuss what kinds of things are on your forbidden list—some of our pet peeves include colored markers, individual pencil sharpeners, pens, colored pencils, and, of course, toys of any kind.

▶ 2. Your policy should include a warning the first time you see something that doesn't belong in school. Students should understand that they have one chance to take the item home.

▶ 3. If you see an item again, your policy will be to confiscate it and place it in your end-of-the-year bag or box. The student will not get the item back until then, unless a parent or guardian comes to school to retrieve it.

▶ 4. Be sure students are very clear on your policy and understand that you mean business. Also inform parents in a note home about your course of action. Your follow-through on this policy will make or break its effectiveness. Once students know you will enforce your rule without exception, you will be surprised at how your problems with these items will diminish.

Sharing time is very special to kindergarten and early primary children. Opening activities allow for objects that relate to a unit of study or something so dear, with valuable language to go with it. A note to parents on the first day of school defines what comes to school. Emphasize that there are toys in the classroom, so parents need to limit what their child selects to share. (Do not allow breakable toys, and ask the parents to have their children express to them verbally what they will have to say about the toy.) Toys stay in backpacks or on the display table until playtime.

Children who do not follow rules relating to bringing toys lose the privilege, for a period of time, of bringing something. Send a note home to request that parents check their children's backpacks before they leave to be sure nothing unwanted goes to school.

If something is taken from a child's backpack or from the sharing table, inform parents by letter that no personal toys will come to school for the remainder of the year or for whatever length of time you decide. Be sure the children are aware of this rule at the beginning of the year.

Rewards

Feeling like Pavlov during a reward shortage? If the rewards you offer aren't the bell ringers you'd like them to be, read on. You don't have to spend excessive time or money to come up with things that are appealing and effective—even for your most challenging students. The first seven suggestions below are absolutely free to you. The next five suggestions illustrate what just a few dollars will buy.

Chapter Outline

- Academic Rewards
- Extra Special Class Time
- Extra Art Time and Extra Gym Time
- Leisure Time Activities
- Lunch With the Teacher
- Good News Phone Calls
- Extra Classroom Chores
- Whole-Class Rewards
- Stickers, Stamps, and Other Goodies
- Coupons
- Certificates
- Tokens and Play Money
- Edibles

Teachers please note: If you are unsure about any reward system—about whether it is appropriate or about whether it can be used in your school—be sure to check with your administrator.

Academic Rewards

Reward students with academic work. Yes, you read correctly. Talk up special activities or projects as a reward for good behavior and sweeten the deal with films, guest speakers, stories, art enrichment—anything you are genuinely excited about will be a believable reward. The best part? Everyone is learning and happy, and, did we mention, it's absolutely free.

▶ 1. Think about a long-term project on which your class is currently working—it could be from any academic area. Then extend that project to include a special activity. If you can't think of something yourself, browse the teacher supply stores where you can find an endless cache of materials and ideas. And here's a tip—you don't necessarily need to bring your wallet, just a pencil, some paper, and some spare time to scan materials you find useful; jot down ideas that will provide you with your special activity.

▶ 2. Grouping deserving students together to work on a special activity, whether it be two, ten, or your entire class, can be challenging but a wonderful learning experience. But be sure you plan the special project with the same thoroughness with which you plan any lesson. Otherwise, it will fall apart, and you will have lost one source of rewarding your students. Also be sure there is an outcome—a product they can display and report on, or the same thing will happen.

▶ 3. Here are a few examples of extending a lesson or project. A study of Egypt could include having a group of deserving students design and decorate a sarcophagus and tell about their product. Find a large box from a refrigerator, for example, to use as the coffin. (You can get these at appliance stores.) Math, social studies, science, reading, and writing can all be part of this activity. For instance, if you're reading *The Family Under the Bridge*, which takes place in Paris, let some students research and illustrate famous Parisian landmarks. Students love to use the encyclopedia programs on the computer or even on the Internet to search for information.

▶ 4. As mentioned, you will need to plan carefully and monitor your group as they work, for this reward idea to be successful and appealing to your students. But once you've hooked them, they'll be begging for more.

Here are some other academic-reward ideas that are fun and appropriate for younger children. Use costumes or props to encourage a group of children to practice and dramatize a book used in a favorite story, a unit, or reading class.

Provide premade pattern books, which one or two children can work together on to fill in the blanks and illustrate and then to share with the class.

They should be very familiar with the pattern, either from a song, favorite story, or a book used in a unit the class is studying. It can be challenging and fun to allow the students to change the characters or ending by providing blanks within the pattern of words.

Riddle books are also very popular with young children—here's an example of a simple riddle book that emphasizes letters and easy clues.

It begins with _____ (letter)

It is _____ (big, small)

It can _____ (hop, crawl, gallop)

What is it? _____

Tape a piece of paper with a flap under the riddle, so the child can color a picture and write about it under the flap.

Another suggestion for younger students is to provide the art materials needed to create a character, animal, or scene from something the class is studying.

Extra Special Class Time

Not a Rembrandt or Picasso in sight as you scan your classroom? Don't be so quick to underestimate the lure of sequins, sticky tape, tissue paper, and lots of glue. Extra art projects can be a real incentive for good behavior—not only around holiday times when your nerves are frazzled but also at less exciting times of the year when you, your students, and, perhaps, your room decorations need a little pick-me-up.

▶ 1. Most students usually eagerly anticipate end-of-the-week special art activities as a whole-class reward. Tie the project into an academic lesson, holiday, season of the year, or just do something whimsical. Again, if you're not creative, there are many excellent, inexpensive arts and crafts books available at teacher supply stores—or even at the library—loaded with simple projects to make using materials you have on hand.

▶ 2. Offering this as a whole-class reward means you need to set up behavior expectations your students must follow to earn the art time at week's end. Be sure your class is clear about these. Entice good behavior by keeping the project a complete secret or by revealing just one or two of the supplies they will be using for the activity. Kids of all ages love guessing games and secrets.

▶ 3. Remember to plan the project thoroughly, have all the materials on hand, and provide enough time for students to complete it. Failure to follow through on any of these will negate the value of this kind of reward. A poorly planned activity, or one that is neither completed nor displayed, offers no incentive for your class to want it as a reward again.

Extra Art Time and Extra Gym Time

Even the most reluctant gym class participant in your group (including yourself) will smile at the suggestion of some extra time out-of-doors or in the gym. Disguise physical education by calling it games, play stations, nature hikes, or contests, and get everyone involved. For almost everybody, an excuse to be outside the classroom for a while and run around is a real incentive.

▶ 1. Always keep in close touch with the weatherperson when you offer extra gym. Have a backup plan if you can't get outside. This may mean you've checked with your school's physical education teacher to see if the gym is available at the time when you are planning your activity. It should also mean you have a contingency plan indoors if things don't work out. Don't disappoint your students, as this reward will quickly lose its appeal if you haven't thought ahead.

▶ 2. Planning is necessary, even for a free-structure activity. Let your students know your rules and boundaries and what you consider inappropriate behavior and poor sportsmanship. If things get out of hand, a fun, whole-class reward can turn into an unhappy, whole-class consequence.

▶ 3. Some ideas for extra gym include a game of kickball (with another class, if possible), play stations (jump rope, beanbag toss, football throw, four square, basketball shoot, follow the leader—take a whistle outside, and have small groups of students move from station to station every 10 to 15 minutes), or take a neighborhood or nature walk.

▶ 4. Here's an idea combining movement and academics—academic baseball. It can be played outside, in the gym, or even in your classroom with careful organization. Break the class into two teams (count off by twos), and have students bat by answering questions you pitch to them. Students actually move from one base to another as correct answers, or base hits, are given. After three outs (mistakes), teams switch. If you are outside, you may want to bring a piece of sidewalk chalk or a clipboard to keep score. Be sure to emphasize teamwork and good sportsmanship during this game.

▶ 5. If you're in the gym, you are in closer quarters and may have to adjust your activities accordingly. Students may have to sit out and wait for their turn. You have to nix suggestions of games that take more space than you have or more physical movement than quarters accommodate. Plan with your class ahead of time, making sure they understand the limitations. Again, a failure to do this will turn a win into a loss for everyone.

Leisure Time Activities

Would a surprising number of your students be shocked to discover there are other ways to spend free time than on television, video games, or movies? Here's another surprise—you may have to be the one to gently lead them to that realization. Expanding your students' repertoire of leisure activities as a reward for good behavior or a job well done serves a duel purpose, but—shhh—don't tell your students.

▶ 1. Reward students with extra reading time. If you have the space, arrange an area of your room with a rug, some pillows, stuffed animals, or even a beanbag chair. You may be able to get an inexpensive (or even free), good-sized remnant from a carpet store if you plead your case well enough. Have some shelves of books close at hand, and it becomes a cozy reading corner. Students can read to themselves, in pairs, or to you or other adults. Inviting younger or older children to your classroom to share books with a buddy can be very meaningful. Making the reading corner inviting and special can also make it an enticing reward.

▶ 2. Quiet conversation or study time as a reward can prove to be very motivating, especially to older students, although some younger groups may be able to handle this as well. You may decide to allow your class to earn minutes during the day—not to exceed 10 or 15—by target behaviors you choose. At the end of the day, quiet conversation, desk games (ticktacktoe, hangman, cards), reading, computers, or quiet study are allowed. As with any activity, be sure you set ground rules. For example, no one should be out of a seat and wandering around, whisper voices should be used, and good manners and sportsmanship must be observed.

▶ 3. Math game stations on a Friday afternoon are a reward to which students look forward. Shaking dice to create and solve multiplication problems, graphing software, creating word problems for classmates to solve, calculator puzzles—all are wonderful ways to reward deserving students, get a math lesson in, and break a monotonous routine.

▶ 4. Free-choice time is another way to help students find leisure activities to add to their repertoire. You can offer table games, drawing, puzzles, activity center projects, or even simple crafts (look in the library for idea books). You must, however, spend time teaching your students how to handle this relatively unstructured time. Students should choose one activity for the entire time; appropriate voice level, good manners, and sportsmanship must be observed. (Note that board games must be taught to younger children in order for them to be used independently and without squabbles.) The teacher (you) must monitor this activity continuously—this is free time for your students, not you.

▶ 5. Remember, as in anything else you do in your classroom, you must have rules and boundaries, your students must know what they are, and you must stick to them. If these are missing, the consequence could be that what began as a reward could end as a never-again-to-be-attempted activity.

Lunch With the Teacher

Never thought of yourself as a popular person? Want a little ego boost? Just suggest lunch with the teacher (you) as a reward. You'll be surprised at how popular you really are. But lunch hour is your sacred time, you say? Giving up one lunchtime every other week or even every week can be worth its weight in gold for the dividends it will pay as a reward for your students. Try it.

▶ 1. You may want to clear this one with your principal first, and ask about a suitable spot to eat. You may also want to be sure it is permissible for students to bring hot or bag lunches out of the cafeteria—check with the cook or engineer. If your students are younger, you may want to arrange for assistance in getting the lunch trays to the specified location to avoid mishaps.

▶ 2. You will need to decide whether the students eating with you will spend the entire lunch hour or just eat and go outside or wherever they are supposed to report. If they remain with you, be sure to have some activities planned such as table games or things they can do for you in your classroom—students often like to help and consider it a real privilege.

▶ 3. You will need to set behavior and manner expectations at lunch. Talking and having fun with one another is fine, but not if they get out of hand. Also, you may want to bring a special treat for those joining you—a cookie or a small piece of candy—but be sure that if you decide to treat one group, you treat all that follow after. Otherwise, you will have problems and complaints to deal with.

▶ 4. You may want to limit the number of students who join you at any one time. No more than three or four may be a good number; otherwise, the logistics of getting students and their trays and lunches to the designated spot may prove too time consuming. After all, it is your lunchtime. Don't end up with indigestion.

Good News Phone Calls

Do the words, "This is your son's [or daughter's] teacher," strike fear into the hearts of the parents of your students? Lower their blood pressure by adding, "This is a good news phone call!" It can be a very motivating reward, especially to those students for whom a phone call isn't usually good news. OK, so Ma Bell charges a monthly fee for phone use—it's money well spent.

▶ 1. The dreaded phone call home can be transformed into a real joy for both student and parent. Be sure your class knows about this reward and that it will be a good news phone call. Talk it up. Remind your students how much their family members will enjoy hearing about good behavior and hard work at school.

▶ 2. You can decide to make these good news phone calls in the evening or even during the day from school to those families where one parent is at home or doesn't mind being called at work. If you are able to make calls from school, you may even want to have the lucky student accompany you to the phone to hear the call and, perhaps, even talk to the proud parent.

▶ 3. You may want to keep track of how many positive phone calls you make per student, and have your class work for a monthly goal. When it is reached, reward the group with a special Friday afternoon party. Or provide individual incentives for those students who need to work harder to get their phone calls—set a goal for a specified number of calls over a certain time period to earn a special treat.

▶ 4. Don't forget those students who are usually always well behaved and successful academically. It's so easy to ignore these children because we are accustomed to their being good students. It means just as much for them and their parents to hear good news. Working with so many challenging students often makes it easy to ignore our little shining stars.

Extra Classroom Chores

Would you believe that the same children who would rather down an entire can of spinach than help with chores at home are the very same ones waving their hands wildly when you're looking for a helper at school? Although chores can be assigned in your classroom (see Chapter 2 under the heading Classroom Monitors and Jobs on page 16), they also serve as terrific incentives for behavior and good work. Hard to imagine but true.

▶ 1. You may have worked out a system for assigning monitors in your classroom for various housekeeping tasks. But there are always special jobs that need doing. For example, you may have some papers that are simple to correct, items to be assembled for a project of some kind, a shelf or drawer needing to be tided, library book shelves that are a mess, and so forth. These provide a golden opportunity to reward someone who has behaved well or performed well academically.

▶ 2. Note that this type of reward may need to be intermittent because you may not always have a project for someone to work on. Also remember that the students being rewarded must be up to the task. If helping with even easy-to-correct papers would be a challenge for certain students, choose something else for them.

▶ 3. Check with other teachers in your building. Perhaps the art teacher needs someone to straighten shelves or sweep up; the kindergarten teacher may need assistance at snack time or during an art project. Be on the lookout for ways students can be of help to you or some other teacher and, at the same time, feel rewarded for a job well done in your classroom. Again, be sure the students are up to the task. If you think they may cause problems in another classroom, find some other type of reward that you can supervise.

▶ 4. You may even want to anticipate special jobs ahead of time or have a standing job with another teacher—one that needs doing every week. That way, students always know there are special things they can work for.

▶ 5. Remember, you want this kind of reward to serve two purposes. Students should feel they are doing something special by helping you or someone else and that it is a privilege. Secondly, it should truly be something helpful to you or another teacher—not make-work. By inventing something to be done, you are making more work for yourself and insulting the student—who, by the way, can usually figure it out.

Here's a fun idea for younger children that can also serve as a help to you. Provide a tub of soapy water and a tub of rinse water on the floor with a plastic tablecloth under them. One or two children can play and, in the process, wash some of the more popular plastic toys. This can be especially helpful toward the end of the year as you prepare to clean your room and store your supplies for the summer.

Whole-Class Rewards

If teamwork brings success on the basketball court, baseball diamond, and football field, why not in your classroom? Even Michael Jordan needed his teammates to win a game. Use this as an analogy to encourage your students to work together each day to earn whole-class rewards. With a good coach—that's you—your team can be a winner.

▶ 1. A whole-class game that takes teamwork to win can be a real incentive. Many classrooms have a Friday Fun activity each week, and the method of earning this reward can be up to you. Why not try a weekly behavior chart where progress toward earning Friday Fun can be recorded for the whole class to see?

▶ 2. Use a large piece of poster board divided into five spaces across the top for 5 school days. The spaces on the left side of the board going down (except for the top space) are for your target behaviors. Decide on about seven or eight of them, which should be areas in need of improvement by your students. For example, if they have difficulty with transitions, you may choose lining up for lunch quietly; if there is a problem settling down in the morning, you may choose quiet morning work time, and so forth. Choose any target behaviors you like, and write them on labels made by cutting 3 x 5 inch cards in half. Attach the labels so that they can be removed, in case you want to change a target behavior.

▶ 3. You will need about 25 game pieces—make a few extra in case one or two get lost. You may want to have the game pieces coordinate with each month. For example, leaves for September, cats and pumpkins for

October, and so forth. Not an artist? Any school supply store sells small, inexpensive seasonal calendar markers. Also, your students may enjoy making the game pieces for each month themselves. Be sure to laminate these for repeated use.

▶ 4. Choose about seven or eight target behaviors. Keeping in mind the inevitable poor performances, recognize that your class team may not earn a game piece for each behavior every day. For a 5-day week, students need to earn 25 points (or game pieces); for a 4-day week, 20 points, and so forth. Be sure to spend time discussing the target behaviors with your students. Remind them whenever they are involved in one of the behaviors where they can earn a point, and be sure to tell them whether or not they have earned a point. Make a big deal out of putting the game piece on the board, and have the board very visible in the classroom. Note that the class doesn't need to earn 5 game pieces each day. The total of 25, 20, 15, and so forth can be in any combination. Each week, the game pieces are removed, and the game begins again.

▶ 5. Don't be afraid to withhold a reward piece if your class performs poorly. If they earn their point no matter what, the game will become ineffective. If the class loses its Friday Fun once or twice, it will usually be enough for them to know you mean business. You and your students can decided on rewards for Friday Fun. They can range from a video to table games, extra art or gym, a choice of free activities—anything you deem appropriate that the class as a whole would enjoy. A word about videos—don't use them every Friday because they will soon lose their appeal, and your principal may frown on overuse. Also, in many schools, only G-rated videos may be shown. Be sure to check your school's policy on this.

 A note to kindergarten and first-grade teachers: Four-, five-, and six-year-olds are just beginning to develop their socialization skills surrounding competition and winning and losing. They may also have difficulty understanding complicated and systematic reward formats, especially long-term, such as Friday Fun. In many cases, most of the children in a kindergarten or first-grade class respond so quickly to compliments, such as singing about the children who are on task or ready to listen and other similar praise, that a structured behavior management system often isn't necessary. A small number of students may need something more. Please see Stickers, Stamps, and Other Goodies on page 81 for suggestions.

Special Note

The Friday Fun Behavior Game is great for encouraging teamwork to earn a reward. But wait a minute, you say, what do I do with those students—and there are always a few—who didn't earn the reward? Here are some teacher-tested suggestions.

▶ 1. Although this is a team game, there are usually a few students in each classroom who are chronic and consistent abusers of your rules. You can't continually punish the entire class for the actions of a few. Here, again, you may want to keep a brief log of the infractions of those students during the week so that they know why they are being excluded. This also permits you to exclude any students who you may feel did not earn an end-of-the-week reward for whatever good reason. If your Friday Fun is enticing enough, you may eventually be able to minimize the number of nonparticipants when they see what they are missing.

▶ 2. You may already have colleagues with whom you've made arrangements to share time-outs, who will take the students who didn't earn the reward into their classrooms during your treat time. Of course, you will be sure to send along class work and a reading book so the students will be of minimum bother. If you choose to do this, you should be ready to reciprocate when your fellow teacher needs your assistance. Also, if your colleague has some sort of Friday Fun, you may be able to arrange to divide up the classes—one week, you take the Fun group and the other teacher takes those that can't attend. The next week, vice versa.

▶ 3. If you choose to send students to another classroom while you have your reward time, be sure to inform your whole class in advance. Students should be aware that they can make their own choices to be a team player or opt to be left out because they've been uncooperative.

▶ 4. You may also want to include students who have not completed their homework or class assignments with the group going to another classroom during Friday Fun. When they have completed their work, they can join in the remainder of the treat time.

▶ 5. What if you are unable to make arrangements with another teacher to take students who have not earned Friday Fun? If you have younger children, you may be able to use a reliable older student to monitor them in the hallway, coatroom, or back of your classroom. You may be able to arrange for an aide to come into your classroom for an hour or so to supervise these students. Be sure to make arrangements well in advance because, often, an aide's time is very much in demand. If there is no one to assist you, find a spot where desks or tables can be turned away from the activities and students can work. Sometimes being in the same room where all the fun is happening can be more miserable than being removed.

Stickers, Stamps, and Other Goodies

If you've frequented any teaching supply store recently, you've probably marveled at the quantity, variety, and varying designs of the stickers you've seen. From shiny to fuzzy to smelly; from very large to very tiny—stickers are made to appeal to all children, no matter what their interests or ages. If you think fifth or even sixth graders are too old for them, you haven't perused the sticker selection lately—and you may find them hard to resist yourself.

▶ 1. Most teachers don't need to be told about the usefulness of stickers for almost any kind of reward. For behavior charts or great reports or projects, elementary school students always covet stickers. Children love to choose from a variety—it makes the reward even more special.

▶ 2. Stickers are not really that expensive. Be on the lookout for them anywhere you go from teaching supply shops to big discount stores—they're everywhere. They usually range in price from about $1.50 to $2.50 per pack. This can vary depending on how fancy they are. Pick up a pack every time you go shopping and, definitely, whenever you go to a teaching supply store—you can find the extra creative ones there.

▶ 3. As mentioned, children like to choose from a variety of stickers. So how do you store all those different kinds so that they are handy? How can you put your fingers on those dinosaurs or those special holiday stickers or the ones that say "Awesome Work"? Here's a useful idea. Most office supply stores sell large accordion envelopes with many pockets. Buy one, and label each pocket with categories such as seasons, holidays, animals,—whatever makes sense to you. Then begin sorting your collection accordingly. Once you do this, you will have what you need at your fingertips, and you can add to your categories as you buy new stickers.

▶ 4. A word to the wise about the huge variety of stickers you will eventually amass. Don't just open your entire collection and ask a student to choose one—unless you can afford an hour away from teaching and learning. Give students two or three (at the most) choices of stickers. For some students, this will still be too much of an option. You may need to be aware of who these students are and limit their choices even more. Or you can use the old, reliable, "I'll count to five, and you must pick your sticker by then." Whatever you do, don't use up too much time over sticker selection, or this reward will become cumbersome.

▶ 5. Rubber stamps are another alternative to stickers. Although they are more expensive, they'll last almost as long as you will, and inkpads are relatively inexpensive and come in a variety of bright colors. Also, various stamps can be combined to create designs or pictures everyone will enjoy. Your stamps can serve a dual purpose and be used for a variety of personal projects also.

Some children in your kindergarten or first-grade class may have difficulty responding with appropriate behavior to the verbal compliments, peer reinforcement, and other cues that are often used in lower grades. These students are the ones who need the instant stickers, stamps, cheers, individual compliments, notes, and calls home about positive actions. Kindergartners are very kind and generous in giving special, positive attention to children that they know are having more difficulty following the rules. Teachers must explain that not everyone understands the rules right away but everyone must help others, who don't, to learn, so the classroom can be a happier place to work and play. Make a special Compliment Book if needed, to motivate those who need more guidance. Encourage the other children to provide a compliment to write in the book. This puts a much more positive light on difficult children rather than having to single them out as students who can't contribute to earning points. Young children do not lose gracefully. They slowly acquire that skill.

Coupons

Does a fist full of coupons give you a feeling of exhilaration as you head to your favorite grocery store? Would you be surprised to know your students will react the same way when presented with them as a reward for good behavior or academic success? Low-cost or no-cost coupons are sure-fire motivators.

▶ 1. Coupons can be used for a variety of rewards from those that are activity centered to tangibles and edibles—it's up to you. You don't have to spend a dime if you make your own coupons and choose rewards that are free. Or you can check out your local teaching supply store for their selection as well as area discount stores for inexpensive tangible or even edible items.

▶ 2. Coupons can be used for an assortment of no-cost rewards such as being a special helper, free time, computer time, choice time, special time or lunch with the teacher, no homework, and so forth—you probably have a list of your own of activities that are coupon worthy. If you want to offer tangible or edible rewards, the list is endless. Buy popcorn, cookies, or pretzels, and let students redeem their earnings at a mutually agreeable time. Discount stores offer many novelties for a dollar or less. There are also catalogues that sell small toys and other prizes in bulk at very affordable prices. Watch for sales at discount drug stores for toys, pencils, crayons, and so forth.

▶ 3. Besides offering coupons on a regular basis, you may find it's often effective to randomly reward students for good behavior or academic success. You can let them know just before an activity as to the kind of behavior or work you are expecting. Another option is to surprise them after a lesson is completed, and reward those who performed well without knowing about the bonus beforehand.

▶ 4. If students earn coupons and choose to save them for use at a later time, be sure names are written somewhere on them in pen or crayon. Many a reward coupon has ended up on the floor with two or more students claiming it's theirs. You may even want to provide a container on your desk where coupons can be deposited for later use, avoiding the possibility of loss or disappearance.

▶ 5. If you decide to create your own coupons, make it a simple task. Use different colored paper for different coupons. Make an original copy to use; then file it away for a later time when you need to replenish your supply. Not an artist? Pictures on coupons are fun but not necessary. Just label each with the reward. Don't have time to cut them out? Reward a student with the special job of cutting out all those wonderful coupons. Then be sure to put them in a safe place where you can find them easily, but no one else can.

Coupons, tokens, and play money can become a huge management headache for a kindergarten or first-grade teacher, because little ones who lose often argue and cry about the fairness of such rewards. Lots of praise and compliments from the teacher and other students along with some of the rewards suggested in this chapter would probably be more successful and appropriate for younger students.

Certificates

Almost everyone has a certificate somewhere, either proudly displayed on a wall or hidden away in a drawer—just can't bear to throw it away. Fancy writing, a big gold seal, signed by someone special—it's a treasure. For students, a certificate can be a very official way of acknowledging their worth and success. Watch them grin from ear to ear.

▶ 1. Certificates are very special and should not be taken lightly by teachers. They should serve as special recognition for a job well done over a period of time, whether it be academic or behavioral. It's nice if they can be awarded at a special occasion in front of peers. This makes it a very important honor.

▶ 2. Certificates can be purchased for a fairly reasonable price or even created on the computer. Sign them, and have your principal sign them to make the reward extra meaningful. You can also buy very inexpensive frames—often for around $1.00. What an especially nice honor for students to receive their awards already framed. If purchasing a frame isn't possible, you can make a simple frame with card stock, poster board, or even colored paper.

▶ 3. What are some appropriate times for rewarding something as grand as a special certificate? Examples of awards include those given for perfect attendance for report card periods, a semester, or even a whole school year; all homework submitted for report card periods, a semester, or a school year; highest report card grades or grade point average; and most improved (which enable students who might not otherwise be able to earn a certificate to strive for one). These are just a few ideas—you'll undoubtedly be able to come up with other appropriate categories that fit the needs of your classroom.

▶ 4. Remember that certificates should be very special and should be given out only at certain times for special accomplishments. They are not like coupons. If you make them highly sought after, students will strive to earn them. Be sure your class knows about them and how they can be earned in your classroom. Plan an awards ceremony; invite parents; serve tea and cookies. Encourage students to be proud of themselves and their accomplishments.

Certificates are great for younger children. You may want to give them out at the end of each semester, and you may want to consider seeing that each child receives at least one. These can be real esteem builders for little ones, and there are many reasons a certificate can be given—the nicest smile; a good teacher helper; perfect, very good, and good attendance—these are just a few of the categories. As your school year progresses, watch for reasons to reward students. Even the most troublesome children can provide you with some proof during the year that they deserve a certificate.

Tokens and Play Money

Who wants to be a millionaire? Well, maybe not a millionaire—but how about earning and saving or spending tokens or play money? Give your students a chance to earn their own "cash" with good behavior or academic success. This idea can be a real motivator as well as a lesson in economics for any age student.

▶ 1. You don't need to spend a lot to use play money. You can design and copy your own paper money, and you can make tokens out of card stock. It might be a good idea to laminate your money so it lasts and can be used again and again. Don't have time to cut out all that paper? Give it to some of your eager students—they'll be more than happy to help. Even first or second graders can usually cut out rectangles and circles.

▶ 2. If you decide to use this method of rewarding students, be sure to decide and even post the kinds of things that can earn tokens or paper money. You may not want to reward every little action this way. Be sure your class knows how they can earn and that they are responsible for their earnings until they can deposit them in your classroom bank or redeem them for rewards.

▶ 3. Also make sure something is provided in which to keep each child's "money." One of the biggest problems with this type of reward is that children often fail to be responsible for their money. It's often missing for any number of reasons. So you should consider the age and general responsibility level of the majority of your students before you decide to use this type of reward. Otherwise, it can truly become more work and hassle than it's worth.

▶ 4. This reward system can be as simple or elaborate as you would like to make it. You can purchase small, inexpensive prizes from a variety of catalogues, especially those that sell to organizations sponsoring carnivals, festivals, and so forth. Students can simply use their money to purchase these items, which are priced according to values you set. With older students, you can run a bank at any level of complexity that you feel your students can handle.

▶ 5. Remember to keep this simple. If you try it and it becomes a big problem, skip it and do something else. As teachers, we need to have our fingers on the pulse of our students—we need to know what they can handle and what they can't. Give this one some serious thought and planning before you decide to use it.

Edibles

Would you be shocked to discover that the word *edibles* when used in connection with the words *students* and *rewards* doesn't necessarily have to mean a mound of sugar covered with chocolate? Food used as part of a reward system can take on many forms—you might even be able to sneak in some vegetables or fruit.

▶ 1. M&Ms™ and other candy favorites aside, there are many foods that your students will enjoy and that you can disguise as rewards. Pretzels, animal crackers, raisins, and bite-sized crackers of any kind are just a few examples of edibles you can purchase in bulk in many deep-discount stores. You can mix or match these to provide a tasty and fairly nutritious reward. Check with your principal to see what your school's policy is on edible rewards, however. You may also want to send home a list of edibles you plan to use during the school year in case some students have food allergies.

▶ 2. Along with the traditional way of rewarding students for their good work and behavior by giving them food, you can use food as an incentive in other ways. For example, make soup as a reward when you've completed reading *Stone Soup*; create something with pumpkins around Halloween or Thanksgiving; have apple treats when discussing Johnny Appleseed; bake your own chocolate chip cookies while reading *The Doorbell Rang* or *If You Give a Mouse a Cookie*. Be innovative, and look for opportunities to combine food with academics. Using a recipe gives added practice in following directions and using measurements as well as cooking and eating the treat.

▶ 3. Plan cooking activities carefully and well in advance. Check with your principal for the go-ahead, and be sure the kitchen in your school will be available, if it is needed. Decide how all of your students can be involved in some way. Be sure you have all the necessary equipment. Write out the recipe, and go over it carefully yourself before you actually make the item with your students. Will you need soup bowls or just napkins to serve the finished product? Anticipate any problems or glitches in advance, for fun and smooth sailing on cooking day.

▶ 4. Cooking projects can be wonderful, whole-class incentives as well as fun activities and tasty (and perhaps nutritious) rewards. Space these projects out strategically during the school year. Make them special and something for your class to look forward to earning—done too often, they become routine and lose their reward value.

▶ 5. Remember, edibles of any type, if used too often as rewards, can lose their appeal. Students become bored with the same old thing, and you may find yourself going crazy trying to come up with something new to feed them. Avoid this problem by using food and food-related projects sparingly. However, interspersed with verbal praise, coupons, tangibles, certificates, and so forth, edibles can be an effective reward.

Consequences

B e prepared. It works for the Scouts, so why not for you? Your reward systems are in place, both individual and group; you use lots of praise and positive comments; you have solid classroom management strategies. But those challenging students just don't seem to be reaping the benefits. That's where the Scouts' motto comes in. For effective teachers, it's a must to "be prepared" by developing a plan that includes options for a variety of situations. Both you and your students will feel more secure if you are prepared to deal with occasional or chronic discipline problems.

Chapter Outline

- Identifying Challenging Students

- Dealing With Mildly Challenging Behavior

- Working With Chronic, Highly Disruptive Behavior

- Support From Other Professionals

- Support From Administration

- Support From Parents

- Support Ideas for Teachers

Teachers please note: If you are unsure about any discipline strategy—about whether it is appropriate or whether it can be used in your school—be sure to check with your administrator.

Identifying Challenging Students

Is a challenging student's behavior just that of a fun-loving, mischievous kid, or could it be more? That's the $64 question—and you're the one who needs to find the answer and quickly. General classroom behavior can deteriorate rapidly if challenging students' disruptive conduct isn't dealt with ASAP. Read on for some useful tips.

► 1. From the first day of school, observe your students in the variety of settings common to your school day. Often, it's easy to quickly identify students who bother others, disrupt lessons, have difficulty with self-control, and are generally uncooperative. You may want to jot down names and keep track of behavior patterns during the first weeks of school. You might find that some students settle down and drop off your list while others seem to continue with inappropriate habits that become chronic.

► 2. Be aware that in the future, you may need the assistance of other professionals in your building to help determine whether a child needs additional behavioral evaluation and support. In order to make a credible request for help, you need to create evidence of a variety of efforts you have made and have documented to change the child's behavior. So it's a good idea to begin early in the year to identify, address, and document the situation. There are a number of things you should do to try to identify the support you've put in place to help the student change behavior.

　　a. Begin a daily anecdotal report on the child. It doesn't need to be anything long or involved. You may want to include information on how the rest of the class is affected by the behavior.

　　b. Think about the positive reward systems you have in place in your classroom, and list them. Comment on how the student responds to them.

　　c. List the individual reward systems you have created for the student. Comment on how the student responds to them.

► 3. Be sure to keep the child's family members informed and involved in your efforts. It is very important to make the family aware of the positive efforts made by the child as well as the challenging behavior exhibited. Coordinate rewards between home and school. Don't forget to briefly document what you are doing to involve family.

► 4. Keep track of the interventions you have used. Perhaps you have moved a child near someone who can disregard negative behavior, ignored inappropriate actions when you could, spent time in class emphasizing the benefits of positive behavior, and so on. Make a list of everything you have tried and the results.

► 5. If weeks pass and the student's behavior has not improved, you will be in a position to use your documentation as evidence of your efforts to help the student behave better. If you have no documentation, other professionals may request that you do the things listed in this strategy before you ask them to assist you. So save yourself some time and tears—take the extra moments to gather the data you need to ensure their assistance.

If you suspect you may be dealing with a student who has special education needs, you may want to consult with the special education teacher or the psychologist in your building. By discussing with these professionals what you have observed over a period of time, you may have a clearer picture as to whether or not the student may need to be referred for special education services. The special education teacher would also be a good resource for help, whether or not the student becomes eligible for special education services.

Dealing With Mildly Challenging Behavior

"If you write on your desk again, you will be spending your recess in here with me cleaning desks." It's a punishment that fits the crime and can be a useful deterrent to future scribbling. Developing a repertoire of responses to mildly challenging behavior is a prerequisite for effective teaching. Here are a few good ideas.

▶ 1. Please note that the suggestions below are for mild disrupters—not those who are chronic and more severe. The ideas listed are usually useful with students who need occasional reminders and redirection. You may think of other strategies; begin to develop a bank of things you can use regularly and effectively. If you are at a loss for a consequence or decide on one that is ineffective or, worse yet, that punishes you as well as the student, or that you can't actually enforce ("You'll stay in for recess for the rest of the month")—you will be seen as someone who doesn't follow through. This could set you up as a target for some of your more challenging students.

▶ 2. Remember the phrase *the punishment that fits the crime* when you decide on a consequence. There are instances where this may be a very strong deterrent to future infractions. Litterers and children who write in textbooks or on others' property present just three examples of students who can clean up their own messes and then do so on a broader scale. These can be very effective consequences.

▶ 3. What about students who speak without raising their hands during a class discussion, who are inattentive, don't follow directions, or are talking to peers without permission? First of all, be sure your entire class knows your expectations regarding these things. Include them in your classroom rules. Before you begin a lesson, go over your expectations again. Compliment those who remember to follow your rules by saying something like, "I'm so glad to see Juan, Karla, and Tanesha raising their hands, following my directions to take out their math books," or whatever your expectation is at the moment. Try admonishing the offender with a compliment such as, "I'm so glad you know the answer, but please raise your hand." Then wait for the student to do so. If the negative behavior becomes chronic, you may want to create an individual reward system where students get credit of some type every time they remember to meet your expectations.

▶ 4. Chronic talkers or those who bother others can be very disruptive to a classroom. Isolation, however, should be a last resort. Perhaps there are one or two students who are able to ignore a talker. Place the offender between or beside them. You might even be able to arrange a hand signal of some sort for the quiet students to use to remind the talker to be quiet. A finger to the lips would be an obvious choice. Sometimes, just spacing students far enough apart can deter excessive noise. Seating a talker near your desk or near a spot where you frequently sit or stand can be helpful. Finally, instituting an individual reward system where credit is given when the student is quiet may work.

▶ 5. Inattentiveness can be very distracting to you as well as your class. Students who are digging in their desk, writing on something, or playing with a toy are not learning. First of all, be sure everyone knows your rules about paying attention. Also, you should already have rules in place about non-school-related materials (see Chapter 7). Take toys away immediately. Be sure there are no extraneous materials on students' desks. Then do not begin a lesson until you have *everyone's* attention. If some are not watching or listening, stop. Compliment those who are ready to learn, and wait for the others to catch on—frequently they do. If you need to stop in midlesson and wait for someone to focus, do so. Use proximity control, or make eye contact. A student who still offends may need to temporarily sit at a spot where there are no distractions, such as a table or empty desk. Again, an individual reward system with credit earned for time the student is on task may be helpful.

Working With Chronic, Highly Disruptive Behavior

Forewarned is forearmed when dealing with students who engage in chronic and seriously disruptive behavior in school. The importance of observing your students' conduct and being alert to increasing problems early on may help you de-escalate some of what is happening. In these circumstances, you may need to seek the support of other building professionals, administration members, and parents. Don't be discouraged. Remember, you can be your own biggest asset in dealing with classroom problems—if you have a plan.

Support From Other Professionals

▶ 1. When you realize you are dealing with a chronic discipline problem, the first thing you must do is admit that you are not Superwoman or Superman. If you have done your best to develop a successful classroom management system, and learning is occurring on a consistent basis, then you are meeting two very important goals as a teacher. However, you can't solve every problem by yourself—and just because you can't doesn't mean you are a poor teacher. That said, your next job is to realize you have allies in your colleagues who can be of help.

▶ 2. Talk to a peer about exchanging time-outs. You may be able to arrange to send a challenging student to another classroom for 15 to 20 minutes to cool down. (This can give you time to cool off, too). You can return the favor when needed. Note that it doesn't necessarily need to be a teacher at the same grade level as yours. Sending a student to a higher or lower grade for a time-out may serve as an additional deterrent to future infractions.

▶ 3. Have a plan for a situation that begins to escalate to a serious level. Develop the plan with teachers who have classrooms near yours, and have it approved by your administrator. Include some of the following things: Who will cover your classroom if you must escort a student out? Who could stay with a problem student while you escort the class out? How can you or a fellow teacher reach an administrator or someone in the office quickly? How soon can someone get to your classroom to help? Where is the nearest phone? Should you or someone else call 911 if it is warranted? As you plan, be sure to keep the safety of your entire class uppermost in your mind. Write down your procedures, and post them in a convenient spot—don't rely on your memory when you may be flustered or upset. You will be much more able to stay calm and in charge if you have a crisis plan in place for your classroom.

▶ 4. Be visible in your school building. That is, know other students beside your own. Be sure they understand your behavior expectations in places such as the hallway, lunchroom, playground, and bus, and follow through on them. Don't let misbehavior in these places slide past you—don't say, "That's not my student." Build a reputation in your school as someone who is fair but has high expectations for every student in the building. Then, when you are asked to assist a colleague—whether it be with a time-out or in a crisis situation—chances are better that the students involved will respond to you in an appropriate manner. Also, other teachers will recognize you as someone they can count on and will be more likely to support you in turn.

If you have a special education student in your classroom, your first line of defense regarding serious behavior concerns should be the special education teacher. To assist you in working appropriately with the student, this colleague will have access to other special education professionals as well as to information from IDEA 1997 (Individuals with Disabilities Education Act of 1997, P. L. No. 105-17; 20 U.S.C. § 1401). Note that IDEA limits the number of out-of-school suspensions a special education student can have. It also provides for behavior assessments and behavior plans to address these concerns. These and other provisions to help teachers should be accessible through the special education staff in your school.

Support From Administration

▶ 1. In dealing with administration members, educators often make two mistakes that are at opposite ends of the discipline scale. They send students to the office too frequently, or they wait too long to get the administration involved. Either of these errors can erode a teacher's credibility as the key disciplinarian in the classroom.

▶ 2. Your students should recognize you as the person in control of the classroom—during good times and bad. Your class rules (see Chapter 6) should be a large part of defining your behavior expectations, and you must make sure to follow through on enforcing them. Every time you send a student to the office for a minor infraction, you chip away at your own credibility as the person in charge. You also risk losing the support of your principal, who may begin to view you as an ineffective disciplinarian. And just like those who heard the boy who cried "Wolf!" the principal may be less willing to help you when you really need it.

▶ 3. On the other hand, serious problems should not be ignored. Even if you have handled an ongoing or escalating situation on your own for a time, make your administrative team (including principal, assistant principal, social worker, psychologist, guidance counselor) aware of the situation. If, at some point, you can no longer control things, the administration should have already been informed of potential trouble. No principal wants a surprise call from an angry parent or an injured student or adult.

▶ 4. It's always a good idea to keep your principal abreast of whatever is happening in your classroom. If you have a newsletter, be sure you place a copy in the principal's mailbox. If you have seen improvement in the behavior of a challenging student, stop your administrator in the hall for a minute and say so. Invite the principal to any classroom programs or special events you have. The more the principal knows about your skills and successes as a teacher, the more likely you'll be to get support when times get tough.

▶ 5. Staff members, students, and parents should all be made aware of the school district's policy on drugs and weapons. Any students found to have drugs or weapons in their possession on the school grounds would most likely warrant a formal suspension from school. After the items are confiscated, some school districts instruct administrators to call in the suspension to children's court, where any further action would be decided. Treat either of these offenses as extremely serious, and do not take a chance by ignoring a toy weapon. It's better to err on the side of caution, and turn the matter over to administration. Be sure to familiarize yourself with the actions your own district takes on these serious matters because policies may differ.

Be aware that chronic, highly disruptive behavior can, but may not always, be an indicator of a child who could benefit from special education services. See the first strategy of this chapter, Identifying Challenging Students, to help you devise strategies and create documentation regarding the student's behavior. Professional support staff in your building, such as the psychologist or guidance counselor (as well as the principal) will most likely ask what kind of things you've tried and what documentation you've made to chronicle the student's behavior over a period of time.

Support From Parents

▶ 1. Make it a point to call parents frequently throughout the school year. Call to introduce yourself; call to report academic successes; call to report good behavior; call families of the well-behaved as well as the challenging students—you get the idea. Of course, you don't have unlimited professional or personal time to spend on the phone with parents. But remember, those calls are one of the best uses of time and money (even free local calls are paid for in the form of a monthly phone bill) that you can spend as a teacher. If you are able to get parents in your corner right away, the chances are that you will have their support when you need it.

▶ 2. A classroom newsletter (see Chapter 2 under the heading Connecting with Parents—Classroom Newsletters on page 13) is an excellent way to keep parents abreast of what's happening in your room. Send your rules and behavioral routines home at the beginning of the school year so parents know what you expect from their child. The better informed families are, the more likely they are to support your academic and behavioral efforts. And again, chances improve greatly that you'll have their support if problems arise.

▶ 3. If a student does begin to have academic or behavioral difficulties at school, contact the family right away. Something may have happened at home that could explain the changes at school. If not, the family will know problems are developing. It can prove to be a mistake not to inform parents or guardians at the onset of difficulties. Children should know that school and home are united and working together in their best interest.

▶ 4. Teachers sometimes say that it is often difficult to contact some parents. Find a way. If you are concerned that students in your class may not be taking communications to their families, try an older, or even younger, reliable sibling. Send newsletters or periodic progress notes home via U.S. mail—your school should pay the postage. If you have a communication of extreme importance, use registered mail—your school should cover that expense also. If there is no phone at home, can the family provide the name of a neighbor or relative with a phone who can relay a message? Is there a work number where a family member can be reached to leave a message or talk for a few moments? Be sure to briefly document any parent communication, including the information imparted and method of contact.

If you feel the need for parent involvement for a special education student with behavior concerns, be sure to consult with the special education teacher. Include that teacher in any parent conference you may plan. Working in tandem with that teacher will ensure that both you and the parent have the whole picture regarding the child and what can be done to help. As noted in Chapters 2 and 8, ongoing efforts on your part to communicate good news as well as concerns to parents help to develop a positive working relationship. This can be especially beneficial should serious concerns arise.

Support Ideas for Teachers

▶ 1. One of the most important things a teacher can remember about dealing with challenging students is to treat them with as much respect and dignity as possible. The reality is that often tempers flare and confrontations occur. But remember, you are the adult. Stay as calm as possible. Yelling or shouting is ineffective. If you feel too upset or angry, arrange a time when you can talk more rationally to the student. Often, a problem need not be settled immediately. You may feel too flustered to make an appropriate decision about a consequence, and as a result, may assign something you cannot implement. If this happens often enough, you will lose credibility with your students.

▶ 2. Accord misbehaving students the courtesy of speaking quietly and calmly to them and, if possible, out of view of the rest of the class. A quiet, calm approach away from prying eyes may go a long way to calm such students and convince them to back away from inappropriate behavior.

▶ 3. Pick your battles. Is it worth a confrontation to make a student with challenging behavior pick up a piece of paper off the floor? Probably not. Is it necessary to stop that same student from repeatedly knocking things off another student's desk? Yes. Save face for yourself and the student by making a wise decision about potential confrontations.

▶ 4. Don't back a student into a corner in a discipline situation. Offer some choices to resolve the problem. This allows the student to see it as a way to make the decision rather than have you, the teacher, make it. Often, that's really what a confrontation is about—who has the power—and you've given some to the student in an appropriate way. Then allow the student some downtime or space to cool off and reintegrate into the classroom without further embarrassment. These actions on your part can often deescalate a potentially serious situation. It's a win-win situation for both you and the student.

▶ 5. Don't peg a student as a problem in your eyes, because that student will quickly gain a reputation in your class—perhaps unfairly. Do your best to treat all your students alike. Although you need to discipline or confront challenging students more often than others, do your best not to let those feelings color the rest of your interactions with them that day. This sends the message that you are unhappy with the behavior not the student. Find something you genuinely like about these children, and concentrate your efforts on helping them develop the positive attributes. This may take time and patience, but it could help smooth the way for improved behavior.

Working with younger children to help redirect their behavior toward the positive should involve ongoing conversations with them as well as regular contact with the parents or guardians. One way to be sure this happens is to have some daily written documentation that can serve several purposes.

With early primary students, it is important to find the positive as well as the negative. You may want to create a format that includes a section for both of those areas. Start with the positive, and be sure you are on the lookout for something good as the day progresses. At day's end, take a few minutes to talk with the child about what is on the daily report. Be sure to compliment the positive behavior and frame the negative in terms of the opportunity the next day will bring for improvement. The student's family will feel more comfortable seeing something positive happening on a daily basis in addition to the concerns you have, and chances are better that you'll have their support in dealing with problems. Be sure to keep copies of these daily reports because they will serve as ongoing documentation for you—and be sure you have a family member sign each daily report. This one little sheet has then allowed you to talk with the child regularly, to communicate with the family on a daily basis, and to provide ongoing documentation for yourself.

■ Suggested Readings

Ayers, W., & Ford, P. (1996). *City kids—city teachers: Reports from the front row.* New York: New Press.

> Students and teachers share problems, hopes, and plans—which is enlightening for readers interested in improving urban education.

Bosch, K. A., & Kersey, K. C. (1994). *The first-year teacher: Teaching with confidence (K-8).* Washington, DC: National Education Association.

> An introduction to a range of topics that first-year teachers have identified as those that need to be addressed, this book is organized practically—beginning with opening-year procedures and ending with closing procedures to finish out the school year successfully.

Dover, W. (1996). *The personal planner and training guide for the paraprofessional.* Manhattanville, KS: Master Teacher.

> This succinct guide provides teachers, paraprofessionals, and all others involved with inclusion, with parameters and possibilities in defining the role of the paraprofessional in the regular classroom.

Faber, A., & Maylish, E. (1995). *How to talk so kids can learn at home and in school.* New York: Rawson.

> This book provides insights into children's emotions, and breakthrough techniques for helping children learn appropriate ways to behave.

Goodman, G. (1994). *Inclusive classrooms from A to Z: A handbook for educators.* Columbus, OH: Teachers' Publishing Group.

> This is a practical guide for teachers as they strive to achieve a working, inclusive, classroom model.

Harrison, A. S., & Spuler, F. B. (1983). *Hot tips for teachers: A collection of classroom management ideas.* Torrance, CA: Fearon Teacher Aids (division of Frank Schaffer Publications).

> Effective classroom management ideas and practical advice are organized and cross-referenced alphabetically.

Mackenzie, R. J. (1996). *Setting limits in the classroom: How to move beyond the classroom dance of discipline.* Roseville, CA: Prima.

> Here is advice on using classroom meetings as a way to teach children to treat adults, their peers, and themselves with dignity and respect.

Moran, C., Stobbe, J., Baron, W., Miller, J., & Moir, E. (2000). *Keys to the classroom* (2nd ed.). Thousand Oaks, CA: Corwin.

> This A-to-Z guide helps empower the new teacher as well as the veteran in creating a positive and successful learning environment.

Murray, B. A., & Murray, K. T. (1997). *Pitfalls and potholes: A checklist for avoiding common mistakes of beginning teachers.* Washington, DC: National Education Association.

> This roadmap helps new teachers avoid many problems they may face early in their careers.

Nelson, J., Lott, L., & Glenn, H. S. (2000). *Positive discipline in the classroom: Developing mutual respect, cooperation, and responsibility in your classroom* (Rev. 3rd ed.). Roseville, CA: Prima.

> Classroom meetings can be used as a way to teach children to treat adults, peers, and themselves with dignity and respect.

O'Donnell, D. G. (1994). *Creating an environment for learning disabilities: A resource and planning guide.* Madison: Wisconsin Department of Public Instruction.

> Teachers who wish to establish communities of learning that encourage students with learning disabilities to participate as full, productive, successful members will find help here.

Walker, J. E., & Shea, T. M. (1995), *Behavior management: A practical approach for educators.* Upper Saddle River, NJ: Prentice Hall.

> Chapters on the principles of behavior modification, methods of increasing and decreasing behavior, psychodynamics, parent training, and home-school collaboration make this text an excellent resource for beginning teachers.

Westridge Young Writer's Workshop. (1994). *Kids explore the gifts of children with special needs.* Santa Fe, NM: John Muir Publications.

> This is a sensitive and thought-provoking look at the gifts of children with special needs as seen by their peers.

Wong, H., & Wong, R. T. (1991). *The first days of school.* Sunnyvale, CA: Harry Wong Publications.

> This top-notch guide helps teachers who want to ensure success in all aspects of their teaching and their classrooms and is a must-have book for new educators!

■ Index